BEYOND THE FRONTIER

BEYOND the FRONTIER

Writers, Western Regionalism and a Sense of Place

HAROLD P. SIMONSON

Texas Christian University Press
Fort Worth

Library of Congress Cataloging-in-Publication Data

Simonson, Harold Peter, 1926–
    Beyond the frontier : writers, western regionalism, and a sense of
place / by Harold P. Simonson.
        p.   cm.
    Bibliography: p.
    Includes index.
    ISBN 0-87565-040-6
    1. American literature—West (U.S.)—History and criticism.
2. Frontier and pioneer life in literature. 3. Western stories—
History and criticism. 4. West (U.S.)—Intellectual life. 5. West
(U.S.) in literature. 6. Regionalism in literature. I. Title.
PS271.S5   1989
810'.9'3278—dc19   89–4411
                                                         CIP

Designed by Whitehead & Whitehead
with
A. Tracy Row

Contents

To the Memory of My Parents

Preface

THIS BOOK expands the range of topics covered in *The Closed Frontier: Studies in American Literary Tragedy*, published some fifteen years ago. I make explicit in both books the central tenet that the western frontier significantly contributed to American consciousness. I now explore at greater length the concept of the *open* frontier, including all its wondrous connotations, and argue the need to recognize its antithesis: the *closed* frontier.

But the closed frontier does not tell the full story either. My later years have convinced me that what we know comes in large part from where we stand—where we live and call our home. To identify such a place as existing between the open and the closed, the light and the dark, the Romantic and the tragic becomes too abstract, too philosophical. Granted that in training our consciousness for both extremes, we try both to enlarge our minds while holding the paradoxes in tension. But a sense of real place, which I associate with regionalism and identify as *frontier synthesis*, offers a different perspective and truth. By having a sense of real towns, ranches, mountains, and rivers—always in relationship to persons—the best regional writers create a sense of home, connectedness and clarification.

I need to acknowledge indebtedness to those persons from whom I drew assistance and encouragement in this study. I want to mention Nelson Bentley, Ivan Doig, and certain members of the Western Literature Association who have sharpened my thinking with their intelligence and wit: Martin Bucco, George Day, Dorys Grover, Richard Etulain, Larry Lee, Merrill Lewis, Glen Love, Barbara Meldrum, Ann Ronald, Helen Stauffer and Thomas Lyon. I especially want to thank Fred Erisman, who is also a member of WLA, for his careful reading of the manuscript and his several key suggestions. More than ever, my gratitude to my wife Carolyn knows no bounds.

Grateful acknowledgment is made to the editors of *The Antioch Review, The Texas Quarterly, The Yale Review* and *Western American Literature* in which portions of this book first appeared.

H.P.S.
University of Washington

BEYOND THE FRONTIER

1

Prospects, Limitations and a Sense of Regional Place

AN INTRODUCTION

For all the controversy raised by Frederick Jackson Turner's frontier thesis, no student of American civilization would deny that the Western frontier influenced the character of this nation. Turner said the frontier was the most important single influence. Other historians have argued for capitalism, Puritanism, North and South sectionalism, or the constitution as the chief shaping influences. Substantial claims support each of the positions. It was the frontier, however, that made America an *open* society from the beginning. Because individuals thought they could move west—because they had a West to which they could move—social mobility became one of America's distinguishing marks. Furthermore, mobility nurtured optimism. In the American consciousness the West symbolized hope; the West figured into the process of civilization, so that the process itself came to mean progress. From this point logic designated the West as synonymous with the American Dream.

Something primal was at work. Once again the old struggle between man and nature took on an immediacy unlike anything Europe had known for centuries. In America this titanic work engaged not only isolated adventurers but a whole society. This fact was manifest from the day colonists first stepped onto the new land. Nature was both friend and foe, and to forget this fact was to place in jeopardy not only physical survival but the human spirit. The struggle, like Prometheus', challenged American resourcefulness and sum-

I

moned American pride. The American became a conqueror of nature, a great rebel whose independence was as sacrosanct as his individualism. He also thought of himself as an Adam, one who merged with nature or, knowing its mysterious power, achieved his full measure through nature. Only as spirit freed itself from the bondage of social institutions and became part and parcel of nature would the individual realize this fulfillment. The West, therefore, held the paradox essential to the American experience. To conquer nature or, in a mystical sense, to fuse with it; to appropriate it for the progress of civilization or, instead, to conform to its ineffable laws for the sake of realizing selfhood; to emulate an Andrew Carnegie or to follow a Henry David Thoreau—this was the American's choice in facing west.

Whatever else the frontier contributed to American growth, it gave people a great myth. As participants in this myth they felt that its colossal meaning ranged from personal and national destiny to human destiny itself. The myth proclaimed that on the open frontier a person could be reborn and have a second chance. Freed from the heavy accretions of culture, the frontiersman again could experience the pristine harmony between self and nature; or, to prove superiority, he again could battle nature's inscrutable ways and, through resourcefulness and strength, triumph over them. This same confidence imbuing the national spirit supported relentless expansionism while assuming purity of motive. By the end of the nineteenth century the frontier was inseparable from national and international history. The real frontier was both a personal and a social process and had clearly become a phase in the American experience. As myth the frontier confirmed political democracy, human infinitude and philosophical idealism.

What then is the significance of the *closed* frontier in history? This is a question Turner prepared for in his famous essay of 1893 but did not answer. He saw his task to establish the frontier's significance during the nineteenth century, not to explore the ramifications of his fateful announcement that the frontier was closed. Others like Mark Twain and Henry Adams knew better than Turner what the real significance of this fact was. Later, so did the Norwegian-American Ole Rölvaag and the novelist Nathanael West. Each in his way knew that the significance of the closed frontier was tragedy. The term was not restricted to a literary mode. Tragedy also meant a way of experiencing American life. This kind of experience touches the national psyche; it affects a people's collective consciousness and, perhaps, its unconsciousness. As metaphor, the closed frontier signaled the kind of American tragedy that destroyed illusions fostered on the open frontier and forced the nation to come of age.

When a nation, like a person, comes of age, it recognizes that limitation is a fundamental fact of life. Painfully, the nation admits that possibilities can only be finite and progress only limited; that solutions to problems are found more often through compromises than crusades. It discards illusions about invincibility and the divine right to exercise power. The nation also abandons the dream that a second chance mollifies responsibilities here and now. Coming of age means awakening to the realities that nations, like their people, are only mortal; that truth comes chiefly through ambiguity and paradox; that the old inheritance of pride still carries its inexorable consequences. These realities emphasize the common bondage all people share and the futility of their efforts to escape it. All this is the human condition, made tragic by the fact that pride and certain illusions live on. In our "universal bondage," says T. S. Eliot, we pretend "to be the uncommon exception."[1] To come of age is to recognize no exceptions, no annulments and, most importantly, no escape from the cycle of genesis and decay. The existentialism symbolized by a closed frontier replaces the idealism engendered on an open frontier. Instead of limitlessness, there is a wall. The tension comes from the illusory prospect of the one and the certitude of the other. Existence in this tension is the heart of tragedy.

But tragedy is not the heart of the matter. The tension between the open and closed, the ideal and tragic may itself lead to a synthesis constituting a new condition—a frontier synthesis manifesting itself in regionalism that conveys a special sense of place. Used this way, the term "regionalism" is

3

not meant merely to suggest a geographic region unique or peculiarly colorful as local literary colorists see it, or as sentimentalists might view it. Nor is regionalism to be interpreted as some imaginative place where a person can escape. Often the West has been seen in such a way. Instead, regionalism is real towns, rivers, mountains and ranches—not as Mark Twain, a realist, or Frank Norris, a naturalist, might see them, but as physical places that one can identify with and connect with inside his own soul. A certain place is thus seen as synonymous with *home*. Home is where tensions are lived out; home is the special place where connections and clarifications occur. In the end home is what brings wholeness and axial centeredness to people, and is therefore perhaps the only resolution any of us can know.

II

In the past the term "frontier" clearly designated more than the western boundary of American settlement, more too than the seemingly endless free land beyond that line. As metaphor the term carried social, psychological and philosophical meanings especially analogous to the nineteenth-century American spirit. Of particular importance is the way the metaphor of the open frontier served the Transcendentalists who preached the limitless potential of the human spirit. But of equal importance is the fact that other writers considered transcendence and reconciliation inconsistent with what Ralph Waldo Emerson called the "lords of life." The point is that Turner's announcement in 1893 did not mark the beginnings of American tragedy, but it did corroborate, as it were, the closed wall as a metaphor accounting for the American limitations.

Emerson serves as an important figure illustrating how this metaphor supported philosophic speculation. As a kind of five-year distillation of his thought, Emerson wrote in his essay "Circles" that our life is like "a self-evolving circle," rushing always outward "to new and larger circles, and that without end." If the soul is "quick and strong," it "bursts" over the boundary on all sides, expanding ever farther. The heart, he says, "refuses to be imprisoned"; for it, there is no "outside, no inclosing wall, no circumference." The death of his son Waldo in 1842, however, severely shook Emerson's faith. Soon afterward he found himself struggling between the ideas of freedom and fate, between the open possibilities in one's merging with the All ("the currents of the Universal Being circulate through me") and the "immovable limitations" imposed by the lords of life.

In what according to critic Stephen A. Whicher is "probably his strongest essay,"[2] Emerson announced the following year in "Experience" that even though these limitations—Illusion, Temperament, Succession, Surface, Surprise, Reality, Subjectiveness—were obstacles, he accepted their "clangor and jangle." Perceiving things differently now from his perspective in "Nature" and "The American Scholar," he shows that experience belies reconciliation, and that wisdom consists in one's living with what he calls "the middle region," "the temperate zone," "the mid-world," where the limitations upon the human spirit find their analogy in a closed frontier. It must be noted that Emerson, not ready to accept a tragic view of life, manifests far less torment in his facing the wall than did Herman Melville. In fact Emerson calls these limitations "beautiful," and then, in what seems more contradiction and paradox, announces in this same essay that indeed "we have not arrived at a wall." He still envisions the time when he might "die out of nature," transcend the not-Me, and "be born again into this new yet unapproachable America I have found in the West."

One might expect that Emerson's expansive design would be more strenuously challenged in his later essay "The Tragic" (1844), but again the walls of limitation—famine, fever, ineptitude, mutilation, the rack, madness, the loss of friends—do not constitute final truth. They create terror and fear only among "imperfect characters." These contingencies are only temporary, just as tragedy is only illusory, belonging to life's exterior. He argues that pain enhances moral purity and that instead of terror we come to know "tuneful tragedy," a condition, Emerson says, "whereinto these passionate clouds of sorrow cannot rise."

Even though Emerson begins this essay with the notable statement—"He has seen but half the universe who never has been shown the House of Pain"—it is clear that he never intended to limit truth to what lies this side of the wall. For all his skepticism, voiced again in his essay on Michel Montaigne—"The astonishment of life is the absence of any appearance of reconciliation between the theory and practice of life"—Emerson's view extends beyond tragedy, beyond the boundaries of evil and fate. Evil, he insists, is merely the absence of good; or, stated positively, evil is good in the making, just as fate is human power that shall be. Fate refines and strengthens human will. "We stand against Fate," Emerson asserts in his essay "Fate," "as children stand up against the wall in their father's house and notch their height from year to year." Giving fate its due, Emerson then transforms it into the means of personal triumph: "calamities, oppositions, and weights are wings and means—we are reconciled." Emerson would have us build altars to beautiful fate and believe that fate is nothing more than an illusory closed frontier that thought will someday master.

With Walt Whitman the exception, John Muir perhaps better than anyone in American literature embodied the search for such altars, if not to fate then to insights reaching beyond his Calvinist upbringing. For him, the Scottish rigor he inherited served purposes his father Daniel had never intended. Whereas the inheritance emphasized the sturdy doctrines of the Church of Scotland—and the father would have the adjective apply also to the way these doctrines were to be practiced—the son followed other ways equally rigorous but far more idealistic in conception and fulfillment. John Muir's was a wonderfully tempered mind, resilient in its openness and yet hard and durable in its tenacity to values that deeply mattered. As for altars, whether as metaphor or reality, Muir was closest to them in California's Sierra Nevada. For all his travels elsewhere, these were the mountains where ineffable things happened to him. His frontier was open to spiritual reality beyond anything Turner imagined and equal to what Emerson experienced.

Insofar as Muir's writings testify to ultimate reality extending beyond culture and human personality and yet having its essence in nature, we may deduce a pantheistic apotheosis at hand. What hedges one from this conclusion is Muir's residual Calvinism which, despite his Emersonian Romanticism, the Californian never completely annulled. To explore such apotheosis, however, is not amiss when considering the way Westerners who followed Muir claimed such triumphant fulfillment to signal not only cosmic consciousness but American consciousness as well. According to critic William Everson, the archetypal American experience takes place in the primitive and mythical West, given voice *par excellence* in the poetry of Robinson Jeffers and such other lyrical gurus as Allen Ginsberg and Gary Snyder.

But other minds have insisted that Dharma intelligences fail to etherealize the circumscribing wall that to Melville represented inexorable limitation. For a person to try to remove the wall, to pretend it does not exist or to strike through it is as tempting as it is fatal. Professor Edwin Fussell points out that to Melville the image of the frontier rarely suggested peace and mediation, let alone transcendence, but rather chaos and horror. After the closing of the frontier, which Fussell marks as concurrent with the Civil War, Melville found himself more desperate than ever. Three years before the War he had published *The Confidence-Man* as a testimony, Fussell says, of a time when "all the values the national culture had been optimistically attributing to the Western frontier were suddenly inverted, and harmony and reconciliation were revealed to be chaos and nightmare." Instead of a trail of truth, the West represented to Melville "a trail of error, a continental mistake, the way to insanity."[3] To support this judgment Fussell refers to Melville's statement in *Pierre* (chapter 9) that in seeking truth too far man "loses the directing compass of his mind"; and as if arriving at the Pole he finds that the needle "indifferently respects all points of the horizon alike." The frontier becomes a chartless metaphysical emptiness. To Melville the frontier also suggests a boundary, an imprisoning wall, and the task of trying to penetrate it is no less than the way to insanity.

Ominous shadowings of this image occur in Melville's early fiction, even though his novels do not directly relate to the American frontier. In *Mardi* he caught the ambiguity of what he called the "boundless boundary of the West," but in *Redburn* and *White Jacket* the image merely suggests confinement and oppression. The narrator Redburn speaks of being "hemmed in" by the darkness of night, as if the black night on the ocean were a great gulf with "beetling black cliffs" all around. A more intense feeling of confinement presses upon the sailor White Jacket—subjected to the law of the Navy from which "there is no escape"; restricted by his jacket, "white as a shroud"; and weighted with all manner of accumulation that the "masoned-up pockets" contain. Only as the narrative ends does he burst from his jacket, which had stuck on him "like the fatal shirt of Nessus," and to what extent he is free depends upon the inscrutable ways of the "coiled fish," a white shark, that brushes by him at that same moment.

The wall with its related images is central in *Moby-Dick*. Melville repeatedly depicts characters who, for all their dignity and democratic worth, confront a superior force or an object embodying power, mystery or injustice. Like Ahab, the prisoner may have the grandeur of a demi-god, yet is inferior in this confrontation. In prolific imagery, unmistakable as it accrues, Melville presents the inferior as one who suffers a grievance or woe, one who is physically wounded, mutilated, dismembered—or immobile, frozen, paralyzed, compressed. What he faces may be a wall, mountain, pyramid, inscription, tattoo, hieroglyphic, scroll, tombstone, picture—typically suggestive of some problem, riddle, secret. He may confront the sperm whale's head, finding it a "dead, blind wall," an "impregnable, uninjurable wall." Or he may fight against fierce winds, wear an "iron crown," uphold "on his frozen brow the piled entablatures of ages," resemble "a captive king," live "enveloped in whale-lines," and typify the condition that all persons share—"born with halters round their necks." Like Ishmael, he asks, "Who aint a slave?"; like Ahab, living in "the masoned, walled-town of a Captain's exclusiveness," he voices his plight, "I feel deadly faint, bowed, and humped, as though I were Adam, staggering beneath the piled centuries since Paradise." And, like Tashtego atop the main truck, he inevitably goes down, the final image that of a "captive form" folded in Ahab's flag (the Stars and Stripes?).

In Melville's evolving tragic vision this image of the wall remains all-important. Resolved to rescue Isabel, Pierre leaves Saddle Meadows and his ancestral house, which at once seemed to have "contracted to a nutshell around him; the walls [smiting] his forehead." The obstacles he overcomes only provide the prelude to the tragic fact that in the end "ambiguities . . . hemmed him in; the stony walls [were] all round that he could not overleap." Using the same image Melville describes Israel Potter, quickened by this tragic vision, as one to whom "the sense of being masoned up in the wall grew, and grew, and grew upon him." Slaves and fetters in "Benito Cereno" signal the same oppressive theme that walls suggest in "Bartleby the Scrivener." Outside the lawyer's window was the omnipresent "lofty brick wall, blacked by age and everlasting shade." Bartleby's window commanded "no view at all," his fate later unchanged in the tombs where the narrator sees Bartleby for the last time, "his face towards a high wall." A sense of "penal hopelessness" pervades "The Encantadas," and the wisdom Billy Budd and his fellow sailors learn on board the *Bellipotent* is that "forms, measured forms, are everything."

Of the ambivalent possibilities for action when his characters confront the pasteboard mask, the blank wall, the closed frontier, Melville most frequently dramatizes two: aggression and quiescence. Illustrative of the first is a movement, often sudden and violent, against the superior force or object. The aim is to destroy it, to strike through it, to penetrate or uncover its mystery. But aggression fails; the blow rebounds and causes self-destruction. Quiescence, on the other hand, is enacted through some variety of endurance, resignation, submission or withdrawal. It allows various conditions of survival (few happy) with any increase of happiness paid for by the loss of independence and dignity. Confrontation may therefore lead, at one extreme, to Ahab's final action and words: "to the last I grapple with thee; from hell's heart I stab at thee; for hate's sake I spit my last breath at thee." Or it may show us a Bartleby, whose doleful refrain—"I prefer not to"—represents the other extreme.

Where in the range of possible action Melville sighted his own direction is less important than where he envisioned the common democratic position to be, represented by the man Melville describes in chapter 26 of *Moby-Dick*. This person is clearly the Westerner whose abounding dignity shines "in the arm that wields a pick or drives a spike," or the common sailor, even the renegade. Unlike Ahab and Bartleby, this person radiates the spirit of equality and is, in short, humanity "in the ideal." In characteristic imagery Melville describes the democrat as one who shares with everyone the "universal thump," the pain and catastrophe and always the limitations imposed by the human condition. Whether seen from "a physical or metaphysical point of view," this condition promises no reprieve or transcendence, only at best the earthly dignity that comes from endurance and endless striving. In one of Melville's great descriptions of tragic beingness, he recalls in "The Encantadas" a night when, lying on his bunk, he listened to the "draggings and concussions" of a giant tortoise on the belittered deck overhead. "At sunrise I found him butted like a battering ram against the immovable foot of the fore-mast, and still striving, tooth and nail, to force the impossible passage."

For all Melville's disenchantment with the nation's westward movement—which, according to Fussell, Melville finally came to regard with "a sense of total irrelevance"—the more important point is that he denied the teleological West.[4] For him the closed wall depicted the world men live in. Human finitude dooms heroic effort to force passage through the wall and to gain universal Oneness.

Like Melville, Emily Dickinson predicted what Turner was later to announce as historic fact. Her spiritual explorations reached distances as great as those Melville traveled, and her metaphysical sense of the closed frontier was just as certain. Overshadowing her faith in Christian transcendence was the constant certainty: "I'm finite—I can't see." In her poem "Their Height in Heaven comforts not," she finds little security in either the "House of Supposition" (the Church and its tenuous doctrines) or the "Glimmering Frontier" that "Skirts the Acres of Perhaps." Speculation about "moments of Escape" in her poem "The Soul has Bandaged moments" suddenly suggests delirious freedom. The long-dungeoned soul, "bursting all the doors," dances abroad and almost touches paradise, only to be "retaken" by the "Felon," then shackled and stapled. Personifying dark mortality, the Felon proves his sovereignty no less than Melville's "feline Fate."

Throughout nineteenth- and twentieth-century American literature the metaphor of the closed frontier and its related images serves this tragic theme. One thinks of Gilbert Osmond's four walls wherein Isabel comes of age; or Jay Gatsby's futile reaching for the green light; or Jake Barnes' cyclic wanderings that take him to Madrid where "all the trains finish . . . they don't go on anywhere"; or the voices George Willard hears whispering "a message concerning the limitations of life." One thinks also of Joe Christmas in Faulkner's *Light in August*:

> Looking, he can see the smoke low on the sky, beyond an imperceptible corner; he is entering it again, the street which ran for thirty years. It had been a paved street, where going should be fast. It had made a circle and he is still inside it. Though during the last seven days he has had no paved street, yet he has traveled farther than in all the thirty years before. And yet he is still inside the circle.

Something undeniably American gives this account its strange power. That the striving to get away only brings one back to oneself is the irony of American exploration, whether geographic or spiritual. Something similarly American is in the names—Jack Burden and Jim Burden—that Robert Penn Warren and Willa Cather give to their respective narrators.

Perhaps the American is J. B., whose Old Testament counterpart knew what it was like to be "hedged in." That the frontier promised freedom from the burden of history was the American Dream. Nothing less than tragic vision could shatter it.

Three writers illustrating the tragedy inherent in the closed frontier—Mark Twain, Ole Rölvaag, and Nathanael West—are not usually associated with the frontier as such. More specifically, Twain's *The Adventures of Huckleberry Finn* and *A Connecticut Yankee in King Arthur's Court* do not utilize the American frontier setting, unless one considers as frontier the territory Huck intends "to light out" to at the end of the novel. The two books nevertheless present frontier assumptions that go to the center of American tragedy. With the prison as the key image in *Huckleberry Finn*, Twain dramatized the conflict between bondage and freedom. The ironic resolution shows that Huck and Jim, both imprisoned in one way or another, are free; whereas Tom, who enjoys freedom from social contumely, is actually a prisoner of the same society. The freedom Huck and Jim know, if only briefly, comes because of their common bondage. Recognizing this condition frees them to love as people, yet knowing that their society tolerates no such love. The metaphor of a closed frontier shows them thrust together, each depending upon the other. Far different from the optimistic self-sufficiency that frontierism fostered, theirs is an I-Thou humanity enfolding weakness and guilt, suffering and self-denial.

Although Ole Rölvaag's trilogy depicts early life on the Dakota prairies, only the first novel, *Giants in the Earth*, captures their awesome magnitude—and this to show the Norwegian immigrants not as conquerors but as lonely exiles conquered by the frontier. Like Twain in *Huckleberry Finn*, Rölvaag was concerned with what happens to people who find escape from personal and cultural entanglements. Rölvaag's great theme is the cost of immigration, and in his three novels this cost is visited successively upon Per Hansa, his wife Beret and their son Peder. In portraying this family as players in a vast tragedy in which an open frontier proved only illusory, Rölvaag struck what he considered the essence of the frontier experience. A people had crossed the Atlantic in search of a new Garden of Eden, only to discover freedom to be a delusion and a curse. Like Twain, Rölvaag questioned the assumption that time and place can create something new. Both writers sent their characters in search of new beginnings, but the truth they discovered was that time and place serve as the stage for broken illusions and human contingencies.

It is with Nathanael West that American tragedy becomes something surrealistic and nightmarish. The westward trek of Americans, growing pathological in their optimism, finally ends in Southern California, a region inhabited by the totally deluded. In West's novels nothing is real. Life is a Hollywood movie set, according to the writer, where make-believe heroes eat cardboard sandwiches in front of cellophane waterfalls. West's first three novels portend the Dantesque world of the fourth, *The Day of the Locust*, in which the mythical journey westward becomes the tragedy of the closed frontier. Iowa folk have arrived at their Promised Land, their Golden Gate, and, finding only California at their feet, they desperately design their architecture to resemble the dream-world that first sent them west. They design their lives the same way. But the existential panic following their boredom and then their discovery that the American Dream is a cheat sends them into mass violence, as if violence alone can satisfy their craving for the fulfillment the frontier promised but never supplied. Violence in West's fiction is not romantic primitivism. It has nothing to do with the kind of natural or even cosmic violence found in Ahab's world. In Hollywood, nature is as dead as in F. Scott Fitzgerald's Valley of Ashes or T. S. Eliot's Waste Land. Violence in *The Day of the Locust* is human self-destruction.

To study tragedy in the mythical West is, fatefully, to consider eschatology. What is the American way of death? Cultural historian Jessica Mitford wryly suggests that American funeral directors have conquered death with cosmetics, and Hollywood's Forest Lawn Cemetery has transformed it into the best of all possible worlds. That euphemism and deceit permeate the American way of both life and death is exactly

13

Nathanael West's theme, for in neither is tragedy allowed. In West's last novel, violence is the antidote for a people's somnambulism. Nothing short of total conflagration will awaken the masses to the fact that death is the wall against which life is lived. Fervently, West's Tod Hackett paints "The Burning of Los Angeles," his own shock of recognition. But the greater shock comes when West unites the art with the reality. Truth is destruction; destruction, truth. The overwhelming irony is that destruction is the truth of the frontier dream. This is Nathanael West's eschatological vision, one that both Mark Twain and Henry Adams had shared half a century earlier. *A Connecticut Yankee in King Arthur's Court* and *The Education of Henry Adams* are works of eschatology. They contain more than a mere longing for the past, so unmistakable in Hemingway's *Green Hills of Africa*, for example. These books by Twain and Adams squarely confront the last things, and it is small matter whether the end comes in violence or entropy, fire or ice.

In its treatment of last things eschatology may not, however, be the last word. Whatever the eschatological impingements may be, the irrefutable fact is that we view them only from and in the present. The present is where we live, and to accept this fact requires no less courage than to envision the future.

It is too easy to equate western American literature with social mobility (western movement) and an open, visionary future. Although a closed frontier including its implicit sense of tragedy provides a necessary alternative view, even this perspective falls short. Somewhere in one's existence must come the recognition that place is itself a present and rewarding reality. To be rooted in place is to know a profoundly elemental relationship that redeems tragedy and futuristic nightmare.

Argued in this volume is the belief that a sense of place restores one's relationship to the land and the community, and therefore to oneself. Despite the disconnection that accounts for our not-so-quiet desperation, the quest for unifying roots continues as it has since time immemorial. According to Northrop Frye, the universal monomyth is the story of loss and regaining of identity.[5] The touchstone of this identity is relationship: I belong; therefore I am. Reviving primitive consciousness that connects us to the cosmos may be the antidote to our anomie. In terms less grand but more telling, finding home makes this connection.

American literary regionalism speaks to this idea. We see how early diarists groped their way to establish the importance of roots which the best regional writers confirm. Serving as examples are three Montana regionalists: Ivan Doig, James Welch and Norman Maclean. Each transforms the commonplace of locale into a sense of place charged with special meaning. Whether this meaning originates from experience shaped by memory and imagination or whether it comes as epiphany, the result transforms realism into as much of the sacred and the redemptive as perhaps we are ever given to know.

To incorporate regionalism into an American frontier heritage promising rebirth is to span the poles of paradox. As the lines of an etching stand out only against the openness of background, so tragedy depicts finite human actions as meaningful only when they contrast with the infinitude of possibility. To mitigate the background is to reduce the intensity of the line; to pretend no background exists is to lose the line completely. From this paradox comes a new frontier synthesis: that the end of our exploring will be to arrive where we started and to know the place, our place, for the first time—to know it as home.

2

Frederick Jackson Turner

FRONTIER AS SYMBOL

THE WISCONSIN HISTORIAN Frederick Jackson Turner was not the first American to call attention to the frontier. The concept goes back to the early seventeenth-century journals of William Byrd, William Bradford and John Winthrop, back to the time when America's frontier was the lush Carolina hills and the rock-bound New England coast. It goes back to Hector St. Jean de Crèvecoeur, whose *Letters from an American Farmer*, published in 1793, announced that on the American frontier "individuals of all nations are melted into a new race of men"; or back to less enthusiastic observers who, like Timothy Dwight of Yale, associated the frontier with unlettered bumpkins. Regardless of viewpoint, Americans acknowledged a frontier early in their history. Thomas Jefferson expanded it with the Louisiana Purchase; Andrew Jackson represented it in the White House; Abraham Lincoln drew his ideals from it; and John F. Kennedy hailed it anew.

But Frederick Jackson Turner, born in Portage, Wisconsin, in 1861, was the first American historian to say outright that the frontier *explained* America. To Turner the fundamental fact in the nation's history was the "ever retreating frontier of free land." This fact, he said, was "the key to American development." People from many different countries came together at the frontier, blending into an American "composite nationality." This frontier experience distinguished Americans from all other people of the world, said Turner, for it gave them an identity separate from Old World traditions. It developed a jealously guarded individualism and laid the groundwork for democracy. On this point Turner was adamant. Democracy, he said, was not imported into Virginia on the *Sarah Constant* or into Plymouth on the *Mayflower* but was born in "the American forest."[1]

Since it was first dramatically announced in 1893, the Turner thesis has been the subject of much controversy among historians. His defenders have amplified the thesis, and many today still think it sound. Others feel that Turner was guilty of dangerous oversimplifications, while there are still others who see Turner's main contribution to be not his frontier hypothesis at all but rather his concept of physiographic "sections." The smoke has not yet cleared, nor is it likely it ever will. The controversy only calls attention to Turner's posture. Every student of American civilization at one time or another confronts the Turner thesis. Professor Benjamin W. F. Wright, Jr., who questioned many of Turner's assumptions, called him "the most brilliant and most influential of American historians."[2] Merle Curti said that in "originality" and "influence" Frederick Jackson Turner "has thus far had no superior if he has had any peer."[3] As the present century wanes the consensus now ranks Turner and Francis Parkman as America's two greatest nineteenth-century historians of their native ground.

It is not enough to say that Turner's fame rests upon his frontier hypothesis without also pointing out the great importance his literary style gave the work. Among the relatively few historians who have actually paid attention to Turner's literary art, none has regarded it as integral to the hypothesis itself. One of Turner's severest critics, John C. Almack, blamed Turner's "unusually happy phrasing" and "charming style" for the fact that readers, deceived by his style, were unwisely led to believe his doctrine.[4] Professor Wright acknowledged his "grand manner"; but, said Wright, Turner's poetic capacity to write brilliant and moving odes to the glories of the westward movement was "more misleading than it [was] helpful."[5] A. O. Craven praised Turner as a "careful, scholarly craftsman in spite of the fact that he undoubtedly viewed history as an art rather than as a science."[6] Henry Nash Smith, both literary scholar and historian, was uneasy in following Turner from a plane of abstraction to one of metaphor and myth, by which process Turner transformed the American forest into an enchanted wood and the frontiersman into a reborn American. What especially disturbed Professor Smith was that Turner's metaphors threatened "to become themselves a means of cognition and to supplement discursive reasoning."[7]

The obvious fact is that historians distrust poetic language on the grounds that in some way it alters and even invalidates scientific findings. That Turner's hypothesis was couched in language supposedly restricted only to the imaginative poet unsettled many of his own colleagues while, paradoxically, compelling them to return again and again to his words. His essays are in fact what the English Romantic Thomas DeQuincey would have called "literature of power." Brilliant imagery, poetic cadences, plus metaphor that becomes epical in its proportions give to his frontier hypothesis a vitality and penumbra of symbolic importance integral to the hypothesis itself.

It is not irrelevant to recall Aristotle's distinction between poetry and history. In the *Poetics* he argued that poetry is nobler than history because the poet is more philosophic, more serious than the historian and because he represents the ideal—what ought to be—not merely the historical or factual truth. In much the same way Dr. Samuel Johnson in eighteenth-century England ranked poetry well above history on the grounds that imagination, for the historian, is not required in any high degree. Just how close historians have come to the level of poetic art is readily seen in Thucydides, Herodotus, Gibbon, Macaulay and Carlyle. Nobody would deny these writers supreme literary distinction.

What has happened since the turn of the century is that history has become a social science. Deeply disturbed by the historian's decline and fall from his place among the humanities, Arthur M. Schlesinger, Jr., describes present-day historical writing as "dry, detailed, dusty investigations, deliberately devoid of sentiment, of comment, and of grace."[8] Left out of his account, however, are writers like historian Robert L.

Heilbroner and social scientist Robert Bellah whose language contradicts this assessment.

This is not the place to argue history's kinship with either social science or the humanities. Turner conceived his task as historian to rest with both. Nothing would deter him from the painstaking discipline required of a historical researcher. Carl Becker, one of Turner's early students at the University of Wisconsin, vividly remembered him coming to class, his immense briefcase bulging with notes after a morning's labor in the library.[9] In Turner's office were to be found population studies, maps, charts of every kind and description, manila envelopes stuffed with notes, all testifying to Turner's insistence that documentary evidence was of unquestioned importance. Yet facts alone never wrote history, and Turner was a supreme writer. As he announced in his early essay "The Significance of History" (1892), the historian's responsibility is to discover the inexorable relationship of evidence. This task presupposes one's finding a continuity to history, an organic and ever-changing life behind the facts. To use facts without making theory was inexcusable to Turner. But Turner went a step further and it was this step that took him into the realm of art, into what Professor Schlesinger has called the historian's "aesthetic vision." Through the welter of facts and theories Turner beheld American society not as an object for dry, technical analysis but rather as a viable organism whose essence could be described only symbolically. Turner's art is not merely those qualities of prose and language noted by some of his readers. It is also his consciousness of society as both unity and continuity and his imaginative power to find a symbol in which his vision coheres.

II

Turner's symbol is the frontier. It is of only minor importance that, taken literally, the frontier signified a "line" up to which population had reached the figure of at least two persons per square mile. Again on the literal level, it is not particularly significant that in 1893 Turner announced the disappearance of a statistical "frontier line." What is important is that in the symbol of the frontier Turner captured the emotions and visions of an entire nation.

Even as an undergraduate at the University of Wisconsin Turner leaned toward a poetic interpretation of history, or, more accurately, he read the poets as the best interpreters of their age. His university prize-winning essay, "The Poet of the Future," written in 1883 when he was a junior, is full of imagery:

> We open the lay of Beowulf, and as we read the poet's page, the walls grow unsubstantial and stretch away in the somber forests and rugged homes of the wild north land; we feel the salt gusts of the sea, the dampness of the wilderness is about us, and we hear the symphony of the wind among the pine trees. We are back again in the fierce, rude youth of our race, of which these songs are poetic crystallizations.

This description suggests a key quality of Turner's mind, namely, the desire to capture the feeling as well as the fact, to return imaginatively to "the fierce, rude youth of our race" in order to understand the vitalism of the present. At Wisconsin young Turner was caught up in Emersonianism and, like the Concord philosopher, declared that man can rediscover the world's foundations, filled he said, "with life, with meaning, with dignity." Democracy, he said, "is waiting for its poet" who will sing "the divinity of man and nature."[10]

What this lofty idealism meant for himself, an outsetting historian, Turner was not long in announcing. In "The Significance of History"—the first of his great essays written after he rejoined the University of Wisconsin faculty in 1891—he set virtually no limits to his task and duty. Nothing less than the "self-consciousness of humanity" was to be his high calling, and in this calling he would summon not only the invocation of the church (*Sursum corda*, "lift up your hearts") but all the "interpretative power" a historian can bring to his work. Turner never repudiated this aim, nor did he ever lose the poetic vision that for him was best exemplified in the high-ringing poetry of James Russell Lowell, Rudyard Kipling, Ralph Waldo Emerson, Walt Whitman, and Alfred Tennyson. Throughout his career the feature Turner found common to these poets was faith in a new order of things, in the democratic ideal, which for the Wisconsin historian meant, above all, faith in the American Dream. "Let us dream as our fathers dreamt," he wrote in his essay "The West and American Ideals" (1914), "and let us make our dreams come true." This dream for Turner was like that of Tennyson's Ulysses—"To strive, to seek, to find, and not to yield." Such was Turner's unflagging idealism, even though a new century was bringing in social, economic and political upheaval that challenged such optimism, and that, at the same time, ushered in new generations of historians sharply critical of Turner's idealization of the American frontier.

Yet students of American history have continued to read Turner. They recognize he depicted the frontier as an epic serving to unify not only the American saga but human history, past and present. At the same time a few readers specifically note that Turner followed the procedure of poetry that, said Professor Smith in writing about the Wisconsin historian, is "to imagine an ideal so vividly that it comes to seem actual,"[11] another way of saying that the *significance* of the frontier was born of Turner's aesthetic vision.

In a remarkable way Turner resembles Henry David Thoreau who chose Walden Pond and its surrounding hills as the place where he would "mine." Turner chose the frontier, "a fertile field for investigation," he said. Like Thoreau, Turner discovered his rich ore to be the existence of vital forces lying beneath nature and civilization and calling them both into life. Metaphysically, Thoreau mined more deeply, yet both he and Turner arrived at essentially the same conclusion about past and present history: history is unified and continuous, and the most fitting image describing it is that of an organism. As Turner explained in "Problems in American History" (1892), the frontier maps he studied in *Scribner's Statistical Atlas* revealed clues to a frontier dynamism. "Perceive," he said, "that the dark portion flows forward like water on an uneven surface; here and there are tongues of settlement pushed out in advance, and corresponding projections of wilderness wedged into the advancing mass." Here was the frontier made synonymous with movement, expansion, evolution. Here on the frontier was to be seen "the steady growth of a complex nervous system for the originally simple inert continent." Out of what Turner called "inert" nature grew a society, a nation, a civilization, all of it a mighty drama unfolding from east to west.

What he saw happening on the frontier was the *process* of civilization—of a people transforming the elemental into the complex, the wild into the cultured, the primitive into the civilized. To Turner the American frontier story recapitulated the story of human history. His monumental essay entitled "The Significance of the Frontier in American History" (1893) transformed the story of simple, scattered localities into the dignity of world history. Something far more than a national story is behind Turner's often quoted sentence: "Stand at Cumberland Gap and watch the procession of civilization, marching single file—the buffalo following the trail to salt springs, the Indian, the fur trader and hunter, the cattle raiser, the pioneer farmer." Nothing less than the mythical conquest of nature is the meaning of his symbolic frontier.

In this essay, terms such as the pioneer's "dominion over nature," his "progress from savage conditions," and his evolution "into a higher state" strongly suggest what was the heart of Turner's frontier thesis. Even though Turner argued, too loosely, that the frontier united heterogeneous peoples into a "composite nationality," and that it served to free the new American from his European past, the real point of both his aesthetic and moral vision was the Promethean struggle to overcome one's subservience to nature and its dark gods. Though for Turner the outcome was never in doubt, the struggle itself first saw the wilderness master the colonist, who, to survive at all, had to put on the hunting shirt and the moccasins, plow with a sharp stick and plant Indian corn, shout the "war cry" and take "the scalp in orthodox Indian fashion." But "little by little" the tide of battle favored the civilized white man—ambassador of reason, enlightenment and progress. This essay of 1893 presents that titanic struggle as the ultimately significant fact in American history. From this conclusion it becomes clear that subduing nature or transforming it to serve one's own purposes describes the American's manifest destiny.

Turner was not yet done with symbol in this essay. Each time the westward-moving American advanced on the frontier, his return to primitive conditions or his encounter with savagery led to a "perennial rebirth; this fluidity of American life, this expansion westward with its new opportunities, its continuous touch with the simplicity of primitive society, furnish the forces dominating American character." To interpret Turner's rebirth symbol is to strike hard upon the other key word in the sentence—"opportunities." First stripped of cultural accumulations, the settler then becomes uniquely self-reliant by developing "stalwart and rugged qualities." This experience is a kind of Thoreauvian "moulting season," an opportunity for the frontiersman to renew his energies, inventiveness, self-confidence, and optimism. Like America's other great nineteenth-century Romantics, Turner vaguely felt some occult power in nature that liberated a person from pettiness and allowed one to grow to full measure. Yet paradoxically it was this same full measure that impelled one to dominate nature. At this point Turner parts company with America's Romantic poets, including Thoreau.

The newborn person in Thoreau's conception is one who, through a process of simplifying, drives life into a corner, reduces it to its basic terms and discovers therein a spiritual reality akin to his own essence. Thoreau's ritual of rebirth awakened him to the mystery of life and to his own participation in it. Walt Whitman's ritual transformed him into a new personality, fresh in the knowledge not only that he was participating in a cosmic design but also that he was the agent shaping it, fulfilling it. No such metaphysical ramifications grow out of Turner's frontier ritual. Instead of mystically realizing selfhood by losing it in the spirit of nature ("I am nothing; I become all," said Emerson), Turner's reborn Westerner is essentially rechallenged—to strive, to seek, to find, and *not to yield*. The challenge is not to simplify but to organize, to utilize—or, to use the word most relevant, to civilize. A new personality does appear but it is not the one Whitman describes in "Song of Myself." It is the Captain of Industry, in Turner's view, who is the flower of western civilization.

It would be a mistake to link Turner with the Social Darwinists, whose view of life contained far more jungle than frontier ethics. Turner insisted that though rude and gross, the frontiersman was not a materialist. "This early Western man was an idealist" who endlessly "dreamed dreams and beheld visions." Turner stated in "Contributions of the West to American Democracy" (1903) that it would be wrong "to write of the West as though it were engrossed in mere material ends." More important, he thought, was the fact that the West fostered ideals of individualism, competitiveness and democratic self-government. Practiced by such western leaders as George Rogers Clark, Abraham Lincoln, Andrew Jackson and William Henry Harrison, these ideals Turner presently saw exemplified in John D. Rockefeller, Marcus Hanna, Claus Spreckels, Marshall Field and Andrew Carnegie. Something of the Westerner Turner found in each: Rockefeller, a son of a New York farmer; Hanna, still a Cleveland grocery clerk at twenty; Field, a farm boy in Massachusetts; and Carnegie, a ten-year-old emigrant from Scotland. Hailing them as "the great geniuses that have built up the modern industrial concentration," Turner was especially struck by the fact that they were trained "in the midst of democratic society." Their ideals were identical to those of the log cabin pioneer.

Of course Turner's successors enjoyed a heyday in attacking this brand of democratic idealism. They saw nothing more in America's so-called forest philosophy than rapacious claimholders employing any means to get rich quicker. Critics accused Turner of ignoring countless issues delineating the new century, including race and class exploitation, suffrage, unions, overseas imperialism and reforms. A year after Turner's death, Professor Louis M. Hacker in *The Nation* went so far as to say that another generation of historical scholars will be needed to correct Turner's ideas, which, Hacker asserted, were not only "fictitious" but "positively harmful."[12]

III

After all the debate, what remains of Turner's frontier hypothesis? No one has yet successfully refuted the fact that the frontier was significant in American development. Moreover, the image of the frontiersman is one that Americans to this day still cherish. But of equal significance is the historian himself, the man whose imagination gave final shape and vitality to the theory and whose imagery brought it to the level of art.

Often overlooked in assessments of Turner is his private agony, much like that of nineteenth-century historian Henry Adams, in seeing the American Dream change into something more violent than he had earlier envisioned. It must be remembered that in his important essay of 1893 describing the triumphant frontiersman, Turner also announced the momentous fact that the frontier was now closed. The reader can hardly miss the tension sustained throughout the essay between the dream and the fact—the dream that to the west would always be a frontier where the American could confront the new and raw environment and master it; and the fact that this geographic and psychological safety valve was shut tight. Just as Henry Adams in the same year viewed America's future in the immense dynamos he saw exhibited at the Chicago World's Fair—dynamos symbolizing the multiplicity and disintegration of the oncoming century—so Turner in viewing a closed frontier wondered what America's destiny would be when the opportunity to compete unrestrictedly for the resources of the land ended and when the restraints of paternalistic government harnessed laissez-faire democracy. The essay's opening announcement, taken from the superintendent of the 1890 census bulletin, that "there can hardly be said to be a frontier line," echoes throughout the essay and, in the final sentence, sounds once more, ominously: "And now, four centuries from the discovery of America, at the end of a hundred years of life under the Constitution, the frontier has gone, and with its going has closed the first period of American history."

Even though Turner took up the study of sectionalism—a form of post-frontier society and culture—and embraced this idea during his last three decades, he never abandoned the effort to understand the American past as represented by western expansion. To him the dates and events were dead facts until the lifeblood of the peoples of that frontier era, their hopes, failures, fears and triumphs, could bring meaning to the chronology of fact.

Turner's writing reflects his own quest to feel and to know the cumulative experience of those Americans who headed west. Underlying the external facts grew the subtle forces of dynamic activity, restless seeking, opposition and conflict, aggressiveness, domination. They gave rise to the raw and sleeping giants of trade, agrarianism and industrialization. Words he repeatedly used—"democracy," "frontier," "expansion," "civilization," "savagery"—have connotations that are themselves accretions of age-old myth and symbol. "Waves of emigrants," "the ever richer tide" of people pouring into the Middle West suggest the waters of the original sea spawning its living organisms upon the land's edge. Routes of America's great rivers become "arteries made by geology." The vestigial remains of each frontier are made analogous to the terminal remains of successive glaciations, and comparing one frontier line with another is like "tracing patiently the shores of ancient seas."

Clearly, Turner's imagination perceived in the American frontier a mythical quality that raised his account far above mere factual description. In *The Interpretation of History* theologian Paul Tillich asserts that "all historical writing which is to be taken seriously must have in it this mythical element," which reaches back into "original epochs" and ahead to "final epochs."[13] This kind of writing demands of the historian an artist's mythical consciousness to interpret the materials at hand in symbolic terms contemporary to the time, the group and the individuals involved. For Americans this original epoch was the dream, its symbolic expression the frontier where the dream could be corroborated. The psychological if not spiritual consequences to a people bereft of both this dream and this symbol signaled for Turner another epoch, perhaps— as with Henry Adams—a final one that Turner chose not to explore.

3

The Tempered Romanticism of John Muir

MOST PEOPLE know John Muir as a keen observer of nature and a wide ranging traveler who became a powerful voice in influencing legislation regarding National Parks and Forests by the end of the nineteenth century. But to understand the deeper John Muir it is necessary to see that behind these activities was a mind at work trying to reconcile conflicting ideas that pertained on one hand to nature that conforms to the mind's eye and projects the drama of one's developing self; and, on the other hand, to nature as divine emanation, as revelation, as typological figures presupposing a distinctly separate and sovereign God. With the first, religious experience celebrates the self as reconciler of all things visible and invisible and the word as symbol of this reconciliation. With the second, the experience sharpens the distinction between the self and the greater infinitude of spirit, and makes praising God an acknowledgment of one's own dependency. For Muir, the dilemma between a Romantic and a Calvinist sense of self had its roots in his studies at the University of Wisconsin and, before that, in his Scottish heritage.

At the university he had encountered Darwinian evolution, including studies in botany and glaciation. Even more importantly, he had read the Concord philosophers and the English Romantic poets. Coincidentally, Professor Ezra S. Carr, who taught Muir the theory of Ice Age glaciation, was a personal friend of Emerson, and Muir's classics professor, James D. Butler, was a thoroughgoing Emersonian. It was at this time that Muir began to take seriously what Wordsworth (whom he quoted often) called the "sense sublime of something far more deeply interfused." It is correct to call Muir a Romantic, perhaps the last important one of our nineteenth-century national literature. As such, he was committed to discover nature's transcendent meaning that he believed informed himself as well. An irony worth noting is that even though Muir's sight in one eye was impaired from an accident in 1867, he emphatically did not have the singleness of Newton's vision that the Romantics decried. Muir's was a transcendental eye that perceived all things material and spiritual in harmony and himself harmonious with all things. Literally hundreds of passages from his books and journals document his search for that sublimity known to the Romantic consciousness as natural supernaturalism. In reading Muir one is constantly made aware that nature to him was emblematic and, moreover, that he would find in nature corroboration of his own selfhood and its salvation.

In sharp conflict with Romanticism and its underlying ideas was the Calvinism instilled into young Muir by his father and the Scottish practice of orthodox piety. Muir recalled with emphasis that his father required daily Bible study. In Scotland, by the time the boy was eleven, he had learned large sections of the Old and New Testament "by heart and by sore flesh." For Daniel Muir, the father, there was no question about God's sovereignty and human sinfulness, nor any doubt about the doctrines of salvation obtainable only through Christ's atonement and eternal punishment for the unregenerate. For the young son the severity of these doctrines was symbolized and reinforced by the menacing North Sea storms, the chill ruins of the old Dunbar castle nearby, and the father's obsessive example of hard work that the rest of the family was expected to follow. Later, as immigrants clearing land in Wisconsin, the father on occasion would say to his son John tending huge brush fires: "Now John, just think what an awful thing it would be to be thrown into that fire:—and then think of hell-fire, that is so many times hotter." The stern Calvinist and Biblical literalist never relented, looking with suspicion upon his son's later scientific studies and regarding his singular passion for exploring nature as sinful. "You are God's property," he warned, "soul and body and substance—give those powers up to their owner!"[1]

Even though Muir's decision to know mountains, not unlike Thoreau's to know beans, was an act of courage, he remained uneasy in not taking his father's dogma straight, and troubled that his conversion to a religion of nature might itself become his literary subject. Again the problem was self. He wanted his subject to be the glorious and interfusing Light of nature—the sovereign Light that transfigures nature when beheld by the eye that itself had been transfigured by divine grace. In relation to this subject his words would be nothing more than incidental, his role as a writer radically subordinated. But Romanticism heralded the ego, the expanding consciousness, the union of self and Light. It also proclaimed, in Emersonian terms, that the artist's words would be God's wine. It was this Romantic faith in the infinitude of self that Calvinism challenged, admonishing that unless the self acknowledge its limits and redirect its celebration toward the wholly otherness of God, the human being stands perilously close to destruction as he declares his sovereignty.

Before we examine what this dilemma meant for Muir the writer, it is instructive to trace Muir's grand commitment to Romanticism. For he was determined to know the Sierra as *his* "Range of Light" and to experience union with this Light. Seeing the Cumberland Mountains during an 1867 walking trip from Wisconsin to Florida, he hinted in his journal what he would feel when seeing the Sierra for the first time. The Cumberlands, he wrote, were "the first real mountains that my foot ever touched or eyes beheld"; and his first mountain stream, the Emory River, seemed, he said, "to feel the presence of the great Creator." But nothing is more prophetic than his description of first seeing the Sierra. He sailed from Florida to Cuba, then to New York, and then to San Francisco. Three days later he set out for the mountains. When still fifty or more miles away he felt their "spiritual power." You "bathe in these spirit-beams," he wrote, and presently "you lose consciousness of your separate existence: you blend with the landscape, and become part and parcel of nature."[2]

Taken from Emerson's "Nature" this description indicates Muir's awareness that paralleling his studies of glacial phenomena was an exciting conversion taking place within himself. About this event the public knew little until 1911 (when Muir was seventy-three) when he published a handful of old journal notes under the title *My First Summer in the Sierra*. To call this a "spiritual autobiography"[3] suggests something of the overwhelming thrill, the sense of joy and wonder that permeates this most remarkable book. In its journal form, beginning with June 3, 1869, the book records nothing less than Muir's spiritual awakening, as well as his incomparably vivid accounts of the Yosemite Valley. Up the Merced River and into the valley itself, which to Muir was like an edenic garden, he beheld sights that left him too excited to sleep: thundering falls, streams, precipices three thousand feet high fringed with trees—"everything kept in joyful rhythmic motion in the pulses of Nature's big heart." Matching the grandeur was the mystery of every hidden cell of a tree, every fibre of leaf and root, "throbbing with music and life." One glorious Sierra day followed another, dissolving and absorbing and sending him "pulsing onward" into what he called true freedom, "a good practical sort of immortality." Stones were "altars," Yosemite Valley a "temple," and he a "pilgrim" amid the "holy mountains." Images of communion, baptism and resurrection tell what was happening to him. He announced his ascent of Cathedral Peak, for example, to be "the first time I have been at church in California." Being baptized three times in one day, first in "balmy sunshine," then in "mysterious rays of beauty" emanating from a plant's corolla, then in "the spray of the lower Yosemite Falls"—by immersion, by pouring, by sprinkling—should convince all Baptists, he wrote to his brother David, "that I've 'got religion.'" He had crossed the Range of Light where now, he said, he should like to dwell forever. "Here with bread and water I should be content . . . the morning stars still singing together and all the sons of God shouting for joy."[4]

That for over forty years Muir repressed his journal describing this remarkable summer suggests that the diary indeed records the unrepressed theme of the awakened self (the transformed ego) and serves as a Romantic testament. The dilemma ever haunting Muir was to abnegate the self, yet to rejoice in its fullness; to write about objective nature, yet to have his words experientially rooted in nature. When he set off toward Mount Shasta in the autumn of 1874 (after a ten-month hiatus in Oakland), he was even more determined to experience the harmony between his soul and the impulses of nature and to entice others to do the same. "Heaven knows that John the Baptist was not more eager to get all his fellow sinners into the Jordan than I to baptize all of mine in the beauty of God's mountains," he wrote. Trudging wearily alone over the braided folds of the Sacramento Valley, he caught sight of the mountain while he was still a long way off. At that moment, he remembered later, "all my blood turned to wine, and I have not been weary since."[5]

To Muir wildness was not a confrontation but a confirmation. To regard nature as an opponent was to alienate oneself from deep sources of identity, to have enmity toward one's surroundings and to make war upon them. He recognized the psychological truth that we pollute and plunder what is separate from us; we protect and cherish what we belong to. Separated, we match our ego against the "other" whether it be land, community, or another person—and in destroying the "other" we break relationships including those supernatural ones that join all to all.

Muir was not guilty, however, of the sentimentality that holds nature as a benign "friend." Such a relationship as this he knew to be fraudulent, its implicit narcissism resulting in the same alienation. Whether in its storms or its serenity, nature was too mysterious, too awesome, for Muir to regard as merely the litmus of his own precious sensitivity. For him nature's forever incalculable wildness confirmed a shaping divinity. That every person also has a wild side, quintessentially incalculable, testifies no less to the same divinity. For Muir the real epiphany occurs when a person experiences the corresponding order between his own deep wildness and that of nature.

II

Muir was determined to discover his real identity in the American West, including its mountains and forests. It was a Romantic identity he sought, one that was part of nature, one that became sacramental by his taking what he called "Sequoia wine, Sequoia blood." Others tried to call him back. After reading the account of a storm-swept night on Mount Shasta, his aging father pleaded, "You cannot warm the heart of the saint of God with your cold icy-topped mountains. O, my dear son, come away from them to the spirit of God and His holy word." Emerson, whom he had met in the Yosemite in 1871, urged him to leave his wild mountains and to become a teacher in some eastern college. Still others who saw this tall immigrant Scotsman with unkempt beard and tattered clothes emerging from the mountains only rarely to supply himself with bread and tea tried to persuade him to stay down, even arguing, as did his Wisconsin friend, Emily Pelton, that he was sacrificing the "refining influence" of society. His resolve remained steadfast. To all who would beckon him downward his reply was the same: "I will not be done here for years. I am in no hurry. . . . I will fuse in spirit skies." His words testify to the unmistakable theme: the paradise to be achieved by the fulfillment of self in union with nature and its transcendent order.[6]

Muir was, he said, "hopelessly and forever a mountaineer."[7] He was also hopelessly and forever a Romantic, driven by the need to assimilate everything into himself and then to write of his own expanding consciousness—to make this his real theme. Muir's problem was not merely the dilemma of scientific objectivity on the one hand and subjective feeling on the other. The deeper problem was what to do with the self. Emerson, for whom Muir cherished a near-worshipful admiration, had said in *Nature*: "I am nothing; I see all." The pronouncement seemed to call for an annihilation of self as the prerequisite for cosmic vision. The real meaning, however, had nothing to do with the transformation that religious orthodoxy described as the corruptible exchanged for the incorruptible through Christ's atonement; rather, it heralded a Romantic enlargement of self, an awakened self that understands all things are part of one's own identity. Romantic consciousness is not one of self-abnegation (*crucis*) nor is it a total absorption into the divine glory concealed behind the images and shadows of nature. On the contrary, the "I" remains sovereign; the currents of the Godhead, said Emerson, "circulate through me." The great Romantic theme is that of self, as enunciated in Whitman's credo from *Leaves of Grass*: "I celebrate myself . . . I dote on myself."

What this means for the writer, as Romantic, is a powerful assertion of self-consciousness. For all his mysticism, the Romantic artist must assert a consciousness of supreme selfhood and transform this heightened sense into artistic vision. He sees all and becomes all through a shaping imagination, a creativity, that preserves, stabilizes, and imbues with significance his experience, and in the end he makes the creation—his own word—ultimate and absolute. Muir would have the spiritual; he was not sure he wanted the literary.

Even though Muir was a prolific writer, he was reluctant to take up serious "book-making," waiting until he was nearly sixty to publish his first title, *The Mountains of California*, in 1894. The truth seems to be that writing for publication filled him with frustration and despair. "No amount of word-making," he said, "will ever make a single soul to *know* these mountains." He insisted that language held no compelling fascination; words, he said, are only "made of mud, for muddy purposes." This deprecation grew from a deep suspicion that going public with words required a certain hypocrisy. "Book-making," he wrote to Mrs. Jeanne C. Carr in 1872, "frightens me, because it demands so much artificialness and retrograding." Something struck him as "not quite honorable" in transforming "raw bush sugar and mountain meal into magazine cookies and snaps."[8]

It is inaccurate to suggest that in publishing his earlier scientific writings in the *Overland Monthly* during the early 1870s Muir wrestled with the problem of his identity as a writer. He was, after all, a scientist intent upon proving the glacial origins of Yosemite and in refuting the theory of cataclysmic origins held by Professor Josiah D. Whitney of Harvard, the official state geologist of California, whose *The Yosemite Guide-Book* was a standard work of the time. Yet Muir, the writer, was anxious about who he really was. Indefatigable as a naturalist and wonderfully exuberant as a traveler, he grew sorely uneasy with the fact that writing demands an assertive ego that first assimilates the world and then imparts it again as an extension of the consciousness that first transformed it. Muir realized to his fear that transforming the world through consciousness and then fixing it into language meant a celebration of ego as the transforming instrument, and it was here that Muir quavered at the possibility, tempting to be sure, that to sing of the world would be to sing of himself.

Unaware of the opposite effect their psychology had, friends urged Muir to write autobiography, assuring him that his books would be "Literature." To Richard Watson Gilder's promptings in 1898 Muir answered, "My life on the whole has been level and uneventful. . . . I am not anxious to tell what I have done, but what Nature has done—an infinitely more important story." This, after years of thrilling exploration. To Walter Hines Page, who also urged Muir to write about himself, he answered in a similar vein: "My life has been so smooth and regular and reasonable, so free from blundering exciting adventures, the story seems hardly worth while in the midst of so much that is infinitely more important." Celebrating his personal journeys looked "too much like having to say, 'Here is the Lord, and here is Me!'"[9] It was the latter that Muir eschewed in his public writing. In his private letters and journals, it was often the only subject.

In a sense the force of Muir's personality made everything he wrote autobiographical. His resoluteness to get as near the heart of things as he could, and to know it as his own, filled his writings with joyful discovery. Books like *The Mountains of California* (1894), *Our National Parks* (1901) and *The Yosemite* (1912), all published during his lifetime, not only describe the then still unspoiled garden of the American West but reveal Muir's reverence for life, for its spirit and secrets. His letters and journals, however (most published after he died in 1914), touch the deeper currents of self, many of them shaped according to the Christian myth of the fall, the redemption and the emergence of a restored paradise.

To examine this level of Muir the writer, whose consciousness spanned both the Romantic and the Calvinist worlds, it is helpful to look at what his so-called Romantic conversion might have meant and to trace his concomitantly symbolic travel. As for his conversion, scholar M. H. Abrams has explained that a conspicuous Romantic tendency was to reconstitute "the stark drama and suprarational mysteries of the Christian story and doctrines" in such a way as to save the "experiential" relevance of the doctrines while making them "intellectually acceptable" to a post-Enlightenment age. What this meant for Wordsworth, who serves as Abrams' Romantic prototype, was a shift from the orthodox view of heaven, Jehovah, and hell to the world within, to the mind of man in the act of finding within itself what will suffice. Accordingly, Romanticism became a "displaced and reconstituted theology . . . a secularized form of devotional experience," an internalization of the Christian drama without "the dogmatic understructure of Christianity" and specifically without the redeeming love and sacrifice of Christ.[10] Unlike Milton's purpose to justify God's ways to man, the Romantic's high argument was the mind of man and all that passed within it. Thus the extremes of hell and heaven, death and rebirth were to have validity in relation only to the self who is both knower and known: the epistemological knower and the ontological known.

The contrary Calvinist notions of a sovereign and wholly other God, and of man as dependent upon divine grace, appear forgotten in Muir's own high Romantic testaments of his newness of being and paradise regained. Muir averred that divinity lies within us as we see everything in nature fitting into us: the sun shining not on us but in us, and the rivers flowing not past but through us. To know in this way, he said, is not only to see a new heaven and earth but to be born again; "as if we had gone on a pilgrimage to some far-off holy land

and had become new creatures with bodies inverted."[11] Thus Muir attributes rebirth to no outside Christological event but rather to the discovery in the mind that spirit and nature are one.

Not to know oneself as part of this unity or to destroy the unity willfully through the ruination of nature—which Muir frequently associated with civilization—is to live a "fallen" condition, whereas to awaken to a pre-existing oneness with nature and spirit is to be restored to new life. Of course, for the orthodox Christian the danger inherent in such Romantic mysticism is not that a person becomes one with nature but rather that he becomes God-like, a dangerous and proud delusion that negates Christ's atonement. About this all-important doctrine Muir observed, in words echoing the apostle Paul, that to many people it is indeed "a stumbling block and rock of offense."[12]

As for his travels, in 1879 Muir's far-off holy land was Alaska. His posthumously published accounts, first written as journal notes, were collected in *Travels in Alaska* (1917) and *The Cruise of the Corwin* (1918). These books depict a more terrifying wildness in nature than described in his California writings; they also reveal spiritual opposites within Muir himself.

His first excursion, an 800-mile canoe trip, sent him exploring the Alexander Archipelago, eleven hundred wooded islands forming the southeastern part of Alaska, with Samuel Hall Young whose purpose as a Christian missionary was to locate and visit the tribes and villages of the Tlingits north and west of Wrangell. Hall's task was to establish schools and churches. Muir's ostensible mission was to study forests, mountains and glaciers. Whatever else he was seeking puzzled the Indians who saw Muir's campfire high on a mountainside one dark stormy night. They asked Young, "Why does this strange man go into the wet woods and up the mountains on stormy nights? Why does he wander alone on barren peaks or on dangerous ice-mountains? There is no gold up there and he never takes a gun with him or a pick. *Icta mamook*—What make? Why—Why?" Why indeed except to verify nature's higher laws. Muir's epiphany came after three days and sixty miles of paddling into Glacier Bay. There, in dangerous waters with icebergs floating everywhere, the two men looked upon Mount Fairweather at dawn, and, in Young's words, "we saw the design and purpose of it all. Now the text of the great sermon was emblazoned across the landscape—'God is love.'" Like Thoreau, who bounded from hummock to hummock, from willow root to willow root on his resurrection day, Muir leaped the crevasses of the tidewater glacier, returning in the evening to tell Young: "I've been wandering through a thousand rooms of God's crystal temple. . . . I was tempted to stay there and feast my soul, and softly freeze, until at last I would become part of the glacier. What a great death that would be!" In Muir's words the whole scene was one of "strange unearthly splendour"; it was a "holy vision." As Young and Muir paddled away, joining the outgoing bergs, "'Gloria in excelsis' still seemed to be sounding over all the white landscape."[13]

Amid these high moments are thematic undercurrents revealing a darker side of Muir's Romanticism. In some respects these Alaska writings contain his most somber reflections. He returned in 1880 for further exploration with Young; then in 1881 he made his third trip, this time as a crew member on the *Corwin*, a government ship instructed, along with its regular duties, to search the Arctic for survivors of the missing *Jeannette* and two other lost whalers. This expedition afforded Muir the chance to see the dreary settlements in the Aleutians, on St. Lawrence Island and along the Siberian coast. Starvation had decimated many of these villages during the winter of 1878 and 1879, and hundreds of dead lay unburied two years later. In some places Muir and the others saw entire villages with not a single person alive, only decomposed corpses still in the huts and grinning skulls "looking out here and there." The flowering plants he was careful to find and note, even on ice-bound Herald Island and Wrangell Land, offer little relief to Muir's other descriptions of gray sleet, screaming water birds, howling winds, the ever-present danger of drifting ice and unpredictable ocean currents. He also witnessed the widespread killing of walruses and seals for commercial profit, and the "butchery" of polar bears for sport. Such killing Muir called "murder," and he was continually baffled that civilized people, "seeking for heavens and angels and millenniums," enjoyed this red, brutal "amusement." The vibrant tone found in Muir's California writings is lacking in *The Cruise of the Corwin*, weighted instead with ironic reflections about civilization and tonally darkened by the omnipresent "black water" dashing against the treacherous ice.[14]

What, then, of Muir's Romanticism? In time he was to learn that more enigmatic than the heart of nature is that of man, and that to fuse in spirit skies does not annul the old enigmas within the human condition. With Romantic bravado he had earlier declared that townspeople were "all more or less sick"— that there was "not a perfectly sane man in San Francisco." Accordingly, salvation was merely a matter of one's fleeing "as from the plague" to purer air. For example, he had written to Mrs. Carr that whereas the tide of visitors coming to Yosemite would "float slowly about the *bottom* of the Valley as a harmless scum," he would inhabit the rocks high above, "half way to real heaven."[15] But later Muir would realize that half way to heaven is nothing more than that. Life still goes on in the lowlands. And he would involve himself in social and political service, enjoy a happy family life with his wife Louie Strentzel Muir and two daughters, become a successful rancher in Contra Costa County, and cherish many friendships. The important point is that later years tempered his Romanticism. The fierce old enigmas were not to be nullified in wildness even if *there* man has his epiphany. The Romantic self assimilates only partial truth at best.

Although he had experienced abounding and overflowing life in which sickness, pain and death seemed not to exist because the self supposedly had merged into something larger, Muir yet heard the bell that tolled him back to his sole self. The fact is that he had a most uncanny premonition of it. The event was his father's death in October, 1885. "One by one we will join him," he mused later, even as he awaited the first snows of winter to fall on his father's grave. The same melancholic thought surfaced in the letter sent his wife a few days earlier from Portage, Wisconsin, where he was visiting old friends whose ranks were thinned by death. "As for the old freedom I used to enjoy in the wilderness," he wrote, "that, like youth and its enthusiasms, is evidently a thing of the past." A new and inexorable note of *memento mori* shaded his reflections. On the occasion of his daughter's fourteenth birthday in 1895, Muir wrote in his journal, "I dread pain and trouble in so sweet and good a life. If only death and pain could be abolished."[16] These are not the thoughts he enjoyed in the high Sierra or in Glacier Bay when death seemed then like some sublime victory, some beautiful corroboration of nature's eternal laws. The faint presence that now looms is not from some far-off holy region but from the grave close at hand.

What lies on this side of paradise reminded Muir of the old Christian dualism between soul and body. In spite of his affirmations about the flow and unity of nature's laws, he retained what Professor Thomas Lyon correctly identifies as a "heavily dualized Christian cosmogony." "Soul and body," Muir wrote, "receive separate nourishment and separate exercise, and speedily reach a stage of development wherein each is easily known apart from the other." Soul was the divine spark known in a rapt state of wildness; body was the bondage of society and mortality, symbolized by life in the lowlands. Muir realized that the claims of both soul and body need to be answered. To turn away from human society in hopes of achieving spiritual purity denied the claims of time and place and denied as well the need for human love. "In all God's mountain mansions," Muir said, "I find no human sympathy, and I hunger." In wildness the soul comes to know a certain weariness that the lowlands, for all their ills, can alleviate.[17]

Revealed in Muir's seasoned thoughts is the ever-present duality between soul and body, nature's wildness and human society, future and past, God and man. His Romantic expectations that in each case the former could become all in all in the latter failed to obliterate the deep Calvinist sense of human finitude and appalling contingency. To soar with elevated thoughts changed not a whit the retributive reminder that sickness, pain and death pervade the only life one really knows, and human love and divine grace afford its only hope.

III

Muir's travels did not abate, but his accounts of them reflect an imagination less spontaneous and empyrean. In 1893 he saw naturalist John Burroughs in New York and dined with poet Richard Gilder. In Concord he dined with Emerson's son, Edward Waldo, laid flowers on Emerson's and Thoreau's graves, went to Walden Pond, and visited Nathaniel Hawthorne's Old Manse. In Boston he saw philosopher Josiah Royce and historian Francis Parkman, and in Manchester, forty miles away, writer Sarah Orne Jewett. He also returned to his old home in Dunbar, Scotland. In 1896 he received an honorary degree at Harvard, and in 1897 another from the University of Wisconsin. For the rest of his life he traveled widely in the U.S and abroad, including Africa and South America. Of all these trips the most impressive was his return to Scotland in 1893, a journey into the past, there to remember the lessons his father had taught him. Still touched by their power, he wrote from Dunbar to his daughter Wanda, "Ask mother to give you lessons to commit to memory every day. Mostly the sayings of Christ in the gospels and selections from the poets. Find the hymn of praise in *Paradise Lost* 'These are thy glorious works, Parent of Good, Almighty,' and learn it well."[18] In what might be called Muir's "seasoned thoughts," especially as they occur in his later journals, there is a Calvinist tone pointing to a world that nature does not symbolize, that a writer's consciousness does not assimilate, that his word can never record. At times this realm is terrifying, other times benign. Mystery is at the heart of it, a mystery Muir frequently called "glorious." Friends chided him for overusing the adjective; the same complaint could be made against theologian Jonathan Edwards. For both, the word signified the ineffable mystery that opens the eye not only to see but to behold: in short, a mystery that inheres in and acts upon men and nature.

For Muir the writer, his closing years, from the time of his wife's death in 1905 to his own nine years later, sent him more and more into the past and into an inner world even while he roamed the outer. His earlier reluctance to write about himself now gave way to a sense of urgency. He applied himself, according to biographer William Frederick Badè, "too unremittingly" for his own health.[19] His effort now was to reach within himself and, using notes written long years earlier, to make public the private spiritual drama associated with that first remarkable summer in the Sierra. He also probed into his boyhood and youth in an effort to understand the shaping influences there. These two autobiographical journeys—*My First Summer in the Sierra* and *The Story of My Boyhood and Youth*—show Muir looking back to a time when powerful crosscurrents of ideas and experiences were shaping his developing self. Considered along with his other writings, these books also show Muir wishing to complete what had always been his great theme: nature, the self, and the divine mystery infusing both with ultimate meaning. Celebrating all three indicated that the earlier cross-currents had never really subsided.

Nearing his end, perhaps he remembered the July afternoon of that unforgettable summer long years earlier in 1869 when he had made camp on the banks of Cascade Creek high along Mono Trail. By the steep waterfalls Muir had observed the little water ouzel flying swiftly amid the spray and thunderous uproar but showing no intimidation from the dizzy precipices. Muir had heard in the thrush's song a message of "strength and peace and joy." When he came to write *The Mountains of California*, published in 1894, he devoted an entire chapter to the water ouzel. By this time the bird had possessed his imagination much as the Catskill eagle had captured Melville's in *Moby-Dick*. Seeing the eagle dive into the blackest gorges, then soar out of them to disappear into sunny skies, Melville recognized a kinship with the human spirit. Even though Muir never shared the depth of Melville's brooding sense of tragedy, something of the same symbolism imbues his water ouzel. In his fuller treatment of it, Muir is struck by the fact that most song birds are silent when wet, but the ouzel sings on through all the seasons and every kind of storm.

Had he lived longer he would have written more of the autobiographical things he had wanted to say. As it was, he spent his ripened days reading old notes, arranging them on the floor, he said, "like lateral, medial, and terminal moraines." The image affords a picture of the interior landscape that Muir was now traversing, still treasuring the longings for communion, the symbols of salvation, and the assurance even in every kind of storm of a sovereign and absolute Power exceeding the reaches of self. On Christmas Eve, 1914, the day of his death in Los Angeles, he was still traveling those moraines. This time they were his Alaska notes spread out before him on his bed. In one of his last journal notations, he had described the nature of this final excursion: "I only went out for a walk, and finally concluded to stay out till sundown, for going out, I found was really going in."[20]

That Muir showed his readers the Sierra more vividly than anyone else has done; that he worked successfully for their natural preservation; that his sense of joyful wildness still provides an antidote for today's desperation make us all his debtors. We are also indebted for his going down into those inner peaks and valleys that call for a different kind of courage. There within, John Muir confronted the essential facts of life and death and demonstrated what it means to be a true frontiersman. Muir reached the edges of experience, his visionary eye beholding all things as linked to one another. Muir had a darker side—a recurring sense of mortality, discordance, and judgment—that intermingled with his Romanticism, deepened and enriched it, and enhanced his searching literary consciousness. The clear Sierra waters, reflecting in his writing a limitless sky, also made their subterranean connections not only with a Romanticist's Walden or a holy Ganges but with the dark and treacherous ocean eddies that swirled around the rocks where Muir as a Sottish child had sat and meditated about his father's Calvinist teachings.

4

The West as Apotheosis

ALTHOUGH John Muir later tempered his exuberant Romanticism, he failed to influence in a similar way subsequent California writers who believed that the West offered still more spiritual harvests. What Muir supposedly had missed was the West as the archetype of America, and the so-called western experience as the American's apotheosis. In this notion rests the fulfillment of the American Dream, to be realized in the holy land of California.

In examining this idea we return to Frederick Jackson Turner if only to emphasize that he failed to push his frontier thesis far enough, stopping at the point where the frontiersman donned buckskin moccasins and took scalps in "orthodox Indian fashion." He said little about the Indians themselves. Too little according to historian Ray Allen Billington, who thought that Turner regarded them only as retarding the advances of civilization, and only as compelling the whites to organize and consolidate their frontier settlements.[1] As for the deeper levels of primitivism Turner did not speculate. The frontier, he said, was a safety valve for the civilized albeit restless American, but Turner did not confront what lay beyond the safety valve. He lacked experience of this deeper world, and was satisfied to say only in theoretical terms that the frontier allowed a brief exposure to primitivism as if this return to ancestral well-springs offered the psychic charge needed to thrust the evolutionary process even higher. Turner saw the frontier as a microcosm where man's history from primitivism to civilization would be reenacted. The pattern itself, however, was inviolable: from primitivism to civilization. Such was to be the meaning of Progress. A little primitivism reminded the nineteenth-century frontiersman of his mercantile errand and martial obligations.

Of course Turner went on to say in 1893 that the frontier was now closed, but he missed the irony in his own announcement. To him and his heroic frontiersman, including the settler and the entrepreneur who came later, the frontier had never been open, not in the full sense and meaning of primitivism. Neither had it been open to the Parkmans, the Irvings and the Twains who journeyed out to have a look at it. For the frontier was not merely a dividing line to be described with demographic statistics, as Turner had theorized it could be, nor was it an anthropological museum of Indian customs that Parkman condescendingly enjoyed examining, nor was it the land of tobacco-chewing prospectors. The point has to do with deeper significances, with levels of human experience that nothing short of the term "mythological" can satisfactorily describe. In this sense primitivism and mythology come together. Whatever Turner and the others suggested about this deeper union, they sadly lacked an adequate vision of it. As for Muir, he captured the vision but drew back from it, allowing his Old World inheritance to shadow the glories that California earlier had blessed him with. Furthermore, he missed seeing the archetypal West from which Turner's West issued. Thus, one could argue that both Turner and Muir missed seeing the real America, even though Turner intended his frontier thesis to explain the very roots of the American character, and Muir testified that the Sierra Nevada were his altars to heaven.

It cannot be said that either man neglected his philosophical homework. Both took important ideas from the Concord Transcendentalists. Even though Turner characterized the American as one to dominate and then transform nature, and Muir held the quite different view of assimilating nature into oneself and thus experiencing private mystical wonderment, both men believed rebirth possible in the American West. One might argue that Muir, who came closer to its realization, hesitated in taking the next step and thereby failed to reach an

American apotheosis. Whether Turner's heroes like John D. Rockefeller and Andrew Carnegie reached it remains moot.

Whether in the paradigm of God-man-nature the human being dominates or assimilates the other elements, the presumption is clear enough: one's sovereign ego encompasses the divine and either rules nature or reflects it. Presuming this, the American is essentially Romantic. To be sure, it is a different starting point from that engendered by the Enlightenment and an earlier Puritanism, both affirming important distinctions in the tripartite scheme.

II

The archetypal West as primitive experience unique to the West is again the question. Again the paradigm includes God, man and nature, but instead of any one having dominion over the others, the primitivism integral to the western experience rules out distinctions among the three. The three become one in cosmic unity. It is this unity, some say, that informs the American character at its heart. "Pantheism," says William Everson in his provocative study, *Archetype West: the Pacific Coast As Literary Region* (1976), is "not only the basic Californian or western point of view, but is essentially American . . . indeed *the* characteristic American religious and aesthetic feeling."[2] So we have still another proposition as to what constitutes the American essence. Here the argument concerns pantheism as the root force, the primal and authentic impulse in the American consciousness. Pantheism, we know, dispels the separateness of God, man and nature: none has separate existence, none has sovereign authority, but each is part of the whole. The ultimate or constitutive reality is the universe, not the Mind or human personality as Emerson had argued. The universe is the All, the cosmos. According to Everson, its microcosm is the West . . . the West as archetype . . . the West as *the* essential American experience . . . the West as true primitivism and myth.

Before looking more closely at Everson's book, something

needs to be said about the Westerner who lived amid the mysteries of the land, sensing in unconscious but collective ways his psychic relationship to it (even though he had never heard of pantheism and would have cared nothing about it if he had). The reference here is not to Turner's frontiersman whose contact with primitivism quickened his self-affirmation and strengthened his resolve to take the land. The reference instead is to the mountain man, portrayed by such novelists as Vardis Fisher, A. B. Guthrie, Jr., and Don Berry and studied by historians and critics alike. As depicted, the mountain man of the Rockies donned buckskins and took his share of human scalps. Although he subsisted on what he received from furs that he trapped, he existed within the deeper rhythms of nature as the Indians had done for ages before his arrival. His concern was less to control nature than to be alert to it. The mountain man was different from the settlers who followed after him because he could hear in nature what others could not and see what to others was invisible. Delinquent in matters of societal laws, he was keenly attuned to nature's laws not only for his survival but for his sense of belonging. A certain mythical heroism colors this interpretation. One knows, for example, that Bernard DeVoto, Ray Allen Billington and Henry Nash Smith have seen the mountain man as daring but degraded, fleeing to the frontier because he was unable or unwilling to conform to social restrictions. Others have interpreted him as the expectant capitalist—hard-driving, ambitious, acquisitive, eager to gain wealth.[3] This pragmatism, however, fails to capture the whole truth about him.

The mountain man *was* a different breed, and the difference lies in the fact that he lived in a world that had not yet been demythologized. He sensed the Indians' consciousness of this pantheistic world and to some degree wanted to make it his own. As for the Indians, he was no more interested in Christianizing or civilizing them than he was in imposing his will upon nature. The mountain man best represents the Westerner who sought to merge himself with the ways of nature and of the Indians whose shamanistic culture made nature sacred. Again, the effort was to experience this other dimension, even to touch the "original" truth, though being wary of ever claiming to possess it. One way was to marry Indian women. Another was to assimilate Indian dress, crafts, art. The most audacious way was to have a *tamanawas*, or dreamlike experience: to go into the forests or the mountains, to fast, to hallucinate if necessary, in order that in a visionary moment some natural object might take on individual sacramental meaning and thus serve as a permanent link between one world and the other. The *tamanawas* became the transformed object itself—a bird, a river, a tree—as well as the religious experience upholding the transformation. In this experience the white man merged with nature and its aboriginal inhabitants. Racial distinctions were dissolved. So too were distinctions between nature and God. The cost to the initiate was nothing less than everything, especially his ego. But the reward was the peace that passes cognitive understanding. This is hardly the outcome that comes to Turner's frontiersman. It is, however, the knowledge that a person exists in a relational world, indeed that existence itself is relationship, not dependency, certainly not separateness, and least of all dominion.

To William Everson the West is archetype. It is the original and unfallen unity. Had he written a longer book he perhaps would have developed his definition and thus balanced the term more satisfactorily with his other key term, "apotheosis." Everson is more intent upon the experience of apotheosis than upon a philosophical analysis of archetypal reality. Clearly, he wants nothing to do with the old God-man relationship in which God is sovereign and man is dependent, nor does Everson find meaning in John Winthrop's famous definition of true liberty as restricted liberty. Hierarchical structure is anathema and non-western. Nor does Everson probe the tragic implications of the sovereign self which wars against God, against moral restraints, against nature; which sees all reality outside itself as antagonistic and all existence as consisting of polarities, encounters, struggles. Everson is as unMelvillian as he is unEdwardsian. In neither does he find what is essentially American. His archetype is a pantheistic West devoid of hierarchy, fallenness, polarity, ambiguity—in short a region "suffused by the presence of the Other."

Everson's *bête noir* is critic Edmund Wilson who, as a thoroughgoing Easterner, showed little sympathy for and even less understanding of western writing. Yet it was from Wilson and his ilk that the western writer had to gain approval. According to Everson, creativity constitutes the power of the West, and judgment constitutes the power of the East. Like a prophet's destiny, the western writer's fate is to stand before the eastern seat of judgment. "Christ left Galilee to suffer crucifixion in Jerusalem. The western artist in New York can expect nothing less." Everson is referring specifically to Jack Kerouac, Allen Ginsberg, Lawrence Ferlinghetti and Michael McClure, but his more important point has to do with the uniqueness of the western experience as being understandable only to one who participates in it. This participation at its fullest he calls apotheosis, the full appropriation of the archetype into one's being. Not surprisingly, Everson associates the Beat and Hippie movements of the 1960s with the western archetype. The beads, buckskins and long hair were its archaic signature. The movements struck at the center of the American experience, and at this center is pantheistic apotheosis.

The word "apotheosis" may remind one of Melville's conclusion to chapter 23 of *Moby-Dick*: "Take heart, take heart, O Bulkington! Bear thee grimly, demigod! Up from the spray of thy ocean-perishing—straight up, leaps thy apotheosis." Or of Brueghel's Icarus plunging into the sea, the uprising spray taking the shape of a crown that heralds the tragic self, still proudly independent even in the very death maw of the sea. This is not what Everson would call a western apotheosis. Rather than the ambiguity of victorious defeat or of what Hawthorne in the *Scarlet Letter* calls "triumphant ignominy," Everson speaks of "gigantic visions," the "primacy of discovery," and, in quoting Josephine Miles, the relationship of "'the gods of the solar system to the gods of the solar plexus.'" In what he calls "the Westward-hungering consciousness," Everson synthesizes a region and a state of being, making each serve the other in a charismatic wholeness, transcendence, quintessential truth and vertical ascent. Western comes to be synonymous with mystical, primal, archaic, religious and cosmic.

In some respects Everson's book is old hat, warmed-over Whitman, exotic Big Sur stuff. But it is also provocative in its strident argument for the western archetype and the western artist as its embodiment. Not the mountain man, definitely not the pioneer, but the western writer is the real frontiersman.

> What attests to it is the scale of imagination, the repudiation of received forms, the eruptive intensity of the energy, the monumental output, the aloof, transcendental passion, the overwhelming pantheistic vision—all these are the unmistakable evidence that the force so long abuilding has at last found its voice.

Everson believes the voice was that of Robinson Jeffers. Joaquin Miller was the archetype's inceptor and Edwin Markham its amplifier, but Jeffers was its embodied apotheosis. Such western writers as Bret Harte, Mark Twain and Richard Henry Dana were only "birth-pangs." In sheer Dionysiac energy Frank Norris, whose *The Octopus* Everson calls the West's *Moby-Dick*, came close to Jeffers. In his portrayal of the artist Presley in *The Octopus*, Norris caught the immensity of the western imagination and mythical consciousness. But after Jeffers, according to Everson, western writing faded into reductionism, with writers like Jack London and John Steinbeck too afraid to allow their pantheistic passion to develop, and someone like William Saroyan too willing to "humanize" it. Ambrose Bierce, H. L. Davis, Walter Van Tilburg Clark and Wallace Stegner achieved a certain brilliance but stand outside the scope of what Everson calls "the primary archetype . . . its protogenic emergence and its subsequent evolution."

Not until the writings of Kenneth Rexroth, Kerouac, Ferlinghetti and Gary Snyder did the archetype once again have its "constellated" voice. For example, in Rexroth's "The Phoenix and the Tortoise" the archetype "rises" to redeem the deracinated intelligence, supposedly T. S. Eliot's legacy; in *The*

Dharma Bums Kerouac "became for a magic interval the archetype's chosen voice." In Ginsberg's "Howl" the dark element introduced into the archetype by Jeffers "thrusts down
to a deeper, more explosive level." Everson's assessment of
Gary Snyder borders on rhapsody:

> Jeffers had looked westward to the vast expanse of water,
> and Kerouac and Ginsberg both responded to the sweep
> beyond, but more than any other American poet Snyder
> has followed that gaze to its conclusion. This oriental
> insemination makes him, among the young, one of the
> most influential poets writing today.

As for Ken Kesey's work, especially his novel *Sometimes a
Great Notion*, Everson finds the archetype with more force
than with any development since Steinbeck. Indeed Kesey's
characters inhabit a vast and forbidding terrain, even though
Kesey denies "the higher register of the archetype, the evoca-
tive pantheism, the sense of transcendental sublimity in the
vastness of Western landscape." Everson thinks this denial is
centered in Kesey's fear of nature: "'That river is no buddy of
mine.'" Consequently, Kesey is deaf to "the religious note in
the Western archetype"; he leaves western fiction "at a point
of impasse." In denying transcendence he has nowhere to cul-
minate his prodigious energies.

The frontiersman today is the artist to whom the mantle of
heroic consciousness has been passed, enabling such a person
to achieve the apotheosis that can awaken us from our spiritual
somnolence. This is Everson's faith. Little matter that the consciousness feels a penchant for violence one moment, a dis-
quieting lassitude the next, and frequently a preoccupation
with death. It need only be noted that California's official
flower is the poppy, that its most popular magazine is *Sunset*,
and that the western archetype has a dark strain, a death-pulse,
which writers like London and George Sterling knew too well.
(Sterling, a poet, committed suicide while Richard Wagner's
music played on his phonograph.) The thrust of Everson's
argument is that certain western artists have penetrated into
the wilderness, there to discover the frontier to be a passage

leading to fuller existence best described as primitive, pantheistic apotheosis. Those who achieve this existence are able to identify the myth of the West with salvation, including their own.

Although not new, this thesis reminds us that primitivism yet resides in the American character despite three centuries of alien ideologies that would work to expunge it. Among the exciting interpretations this fact elicits, one must be the centrality of the western experience as representing sublime wholeness. A corollary suggests that this wholeness is our destiny, to be reached not in going along the upward way charted by social evolutionists but by going back to truths rooted in primitive consciousness. Unfortunately, the nagging problem Everson fails to recognize is that, like one's hearing a fly buzz at the moment of transcendence, even the most rapturous vision emanating from primitive consciousness never completely expunges America's other inheritances, including the shadows of tragedy emanating from Athens and Jerusalem, slicing through the western archetype, and darkening the apotheosis.

5

The Closed Frontier and American Tragedy

FREDERICK JACKSON TURNER restated what American visionaries before him had dreamed about. The colonists had seen a profoundly Biblical significance in their work. As Perry Miller, the premier scholar of American Puritanism, put it, their mission was an "errand into the wilderness," there to undergo punitive testing and to find providential reward. They were the chosen people, their hope millennial, their land a "New English Canaan." To Thomas Morton New England's summer beauty made the land "seem paradise." Increase Mather thought it a Kingdom of Christ "restored to its Paradise state."[1] Towns bearing such names as Harmony, Concord, New Hope and Zion clearly indicated the sense of destiny that the American, as a new Adam, felt. In studying this visionary spirit, theologian H. Richard Niebuhr cogently titled his book *The Kingdom of God in America*.

Long before William Everson's California gurus, nineteenth century Americans had seen "the apotheosis of Adam";[2] this was the century of America's great westward expansion. While Emerson in Concord was saying that "our day of dependence, our long apprenticeship to the learning of other lands, draws to a close" ("The American Scholar"), James Fenimore Cooper's Natty Bumppo had already demonstrated to what epical proportions the frontiersman could grow. While Thoreau was saying in *Walden* that the dawn of this new day will make our present sun as but a morning star, and while Whitman sang of himself as an ever-growing, ever-enlarging personality that "fillest the vastnesses of Space" ("Passage to India"), out on the frontier the Daniel Boones and Davy Crocketts had acted

53

upon this new faith. In his book *The Oregon Trail* (1849), Francis Parkman used the term "jumping off" to describe the pioneers' departure, many of them from that town in Missouri auspiciously called Independence.

Jumping off meant keeping ahead of oppressive complexities. It meant separation from the past, new adventure, new history, new being. It meant the American Dream, a virgin land, a golden gate, an open road. In short, it meant Eden. "The Edenic myth," writes critic Charles L. Sanford in *The Quest for Paradise*, "has been the most powerful and comprehensive organizing force in American culture."[3] To nineteenth-century America every individual was as new as Adam. Each was the first man, each the new unfallen. The American experience was like a molting season, a gradual sloughing of the old skin. In philosophic terms the American frontier experience was idealism that stretched out into mysticism. In "The Significance of the Frontier in American History," Turner called it "a gate of escape from the bondage of the past"—the bondage not only of history and institutions but also of human finitude itself. A wall had been broken, a door opened. Out beyond lay a land where "waters ran clear . . . free grass waved a carpet over the face of the earth, and America's man on horseback . . . rode over the rim with all the abandon, energy, insolence, pride, carelessness, and confidence epitomizing the becoming West."[4]

Turner's 1893 essay is doubly important, however, for in it he made the immensely critical point that the frontier was now closed. No land now remained to be designated unsettled. Therefore, that vaguely determined line—the frontier—had vanished. More importantly, with the closing of the frontier came the end of the American myth.

Turner failed to comprehend the full weight of this truth. Actually he thought that even with the frontier closed its old spirit would remain alive; and so in later writing he hailed John D. Rockefeller, Andrew Carnegie, and all other Horatio Algers who, in Turner's view, professed the concomitants to frontierism: free enterprise, laissez-faire, individual rights, natural rights, manifest destiny, popular nationalism and social mobility. Yet there is something unmistakably ominous in the way Turner begins this essay, first by quoting the census report of 1890 and then by suggesting that this report "marks the closing of a great historic movement." He concludes the essay even more gravely by pointing out that the closed frontier now signals the end of an era that started four centuries earlier with the discovery of America and a hundred years earlier with the Constitution. Indeed, Turner knew America was at a crucial point, but his inveterate optimism shielded him from the tragic sense that darkened Henry Adams' prophetic vision. Nevertheless Turner's announcement suggested that the West was no longer another Eden, the Westerner no longer another Adam. The immense implications of an open frontier were now to be eclipsed by those of a closed one. The metaphor changed from endless space to solid wall. Epic changed to tragedy.

The central point regarding the closed frontier is that from this condition develops the necessary climate for tragedy—specifically, for American tragedy. What a closed frontier implies obviously touches other terms by which Americans have sought to understand their development. One thinks, for example, of Adams' symbolic Virgin and Dynamo, or in more recent years of Henry Nash Smith's symbolic Garden and Desert. Henry Steele Commager described the decade of the nineties as "the watershed of American history." Henry F. May called the years 1912 to 1917 "the end of American innocence." Van Wyck Brooks used the image of Indian summer, and Leo Marx, in his book suggestively called *The Machine in the Garden*, indicated technology as still another way this important transition in the American experience came about.[5]

What all these terms, including that of a closed frontier, suggest is the end of the Edenic myth and the illusions it fostered. Youth is a time for these illusions, but maturity brings the old truths about the tragedy of great expectations. An open frontier was the perfect setting for youthful ambition, for the proud confidence that anything undertaken could be victoriously completed. It was also the place where those breathtaking ideas about the American Adam could be dramatized and where a new birth of frontier freedom promised an end not only to the bondage of tradition but to the age-old curse of original sin. What need was there in America for the myth of Adam's fall when Emerson in his monumental essay "Nature" assured his countrymen that through mind alone they could build their own world? "As fast as you conform your life to the pure ideas in your mind," he said, "that will unfold its great proportions." All things disagreeable—"swine, spiders, snakes, pests, madhouses, prisons, enemies"—will vanish until "evil is no more seen." On the other hand Melville, Hawthorne and James understood the nature of tragedy because they also understood that human evil is not to be annulled by Emersonian idealism.

II

There was little inclination among nineteenth-century Americans to think about tragedy. With an open frontier and its still viable myth, Americans concurred with Thoreau, who in "Civil Disobedience" reported about his one night in a Concord jail, "I did not for a moment feel confined, and the walls seemed a great waste of stone and mortar." The spirit of the day was one of expansion: a fervent belief that all things were possible—that, for example, Americans could attain eternity, become spirit and find truth. Whether one's philosophy rested in the idealism of Emerson or the social evolutionism of Herbert Spencer, Americans confidently looked ahead to a time when human problems would disappear and ethics triumph.

Today's American Dream appears in television advertising and slick magazine pages. Answers to problems require only that we buy the large economy-sized package. A holiday cruise promises escape from the treadmill. Hair dyes and diets restore our lost youth. Believing that nothing can frustrate us in the West, we still trek to California, there in the land of sunshine and orange blossoms to find the utopia for which in Iowa we saved our dollars and stock certificates. We attend the Hollywood churches novelist Nathanael West describes in *The Day of the Locust*: the "Church of Christ, Physical," where holiness comes through the use of chest weights and spring grips; the "Church Invisible," where fortunes are told and the dead find lost objects; the "Tabernacle of the Third Coming," where a woman dressed as a man preaches the "Crusade Against Salt"; and the "Temple Moderne," under whose roof "Brain-Breathing, the Secret of the Aztecs," is taught. And we hear not a word about sin.

Nathanael West's satire on cultists and pathological optimists calls up the peculiarly American penchant for supernaturalism, whether as mysticism, Emersonian transcendentalism, Mary Baker Eddy's Christian Science, or William Everson's California apotheosis. It is important to remember our indebtedness in the nineteenth century to Oriental philosophy with its antipathy toward tragedy. Believing in a symbolically open frontier meant, therefore, transcending human finitude and traveling into those mysterious and supernatural realms beyond this life of clay. It also came to mean a denial of physical reality itself. Mrs. Eddy's statement in 1875 proclaimed that there is neither "life, truth, intelligence, nor substance in matter."[6] By contrast tragedy concerns itself not with the invisible world of mystic, saint or swami, but with the visible world of prisoner and slave. "Who aint a slave? Tell me that," asks Melville's Ishmael. It is a world resembling "a cramped cell," writes Spanish existentialist Miguel de Unamuno, "against the bars of which my soul beats its wings in vain." We look out and wish "to merge . . . with the totality of things visible and invisible, to extend [ourselves] into the illimitable of space and to prolong [ourselves] into the infinite of time."[7] But our tragic condition resounds with an everlasting "No."

Even after the slaughter of World War I, when it seemed self-evident that something had gone wrong in human affairs, religious liberals in America were determined to muffle this "No." Influenced by new findings in Biblical criticism, history of religions, and the psychology of religion, they generally supported the view that Biblical history was itself a movement toward lofty ethical monotheism. They also accepted the nineteenth-century doctrine of progress that was handily supported by the theory of evolution. The logical step was then to affirm the great moral possibilities of humanity. Any suggestion that original sin might limit these possibilities was put aside. "If you told the modern American that he is totally depraved," said Santayana in 1911, "he would think you were joking, as he himself usually is. He is convinced that he always has been, and always will be, victorious and blameless."[8] If anything, the war corroborated this judgment, and American religious liberals under the banner of theologian Walter Rauschenbusch went forth to spread the socialized gospel of Christian love. Not until Reinhold Niebuhr came onto the scene were the optimistic assumptions of Protestant liberalism successfully challenged.

As for the young artists and intellectuals, their escape from all that a closed frontier implied left them foundering. Some went to Europe where no frontier dream existed. Some simply moved away from their home towns and the puerile Babbittry stifling them. Others went to Greenwich Village in New York or established colonies at Grantwood and Provincetown. Some took up Spiritualism in California's City of Angels. The period has somber personal importance too. Vachel Lindsay committed suicide in 1932; F. Scott Fitzgerald cracked up in the late thirties. In the forties Ezra Pound was spared facing trial for treason only because he was judged mentally unsound. John Gould Fletcher committed suicide in 1950; Ernest Hemingway, in 1961; Sylvia Plath two years later; John Berryman, in 1972. The case of Eugene O'Neill may also figure in here, but more testimonial is that of his son, Eugene, a tall, black-haired man standing six feet three, at 215 pounds, with a booming voice and a black beard, professor of English at Yale and classical scholar, who in 1950, at the age of thirty-nine, still slept with a teddy bear of childhood days. That same year he committed suicide with a razor.[9]

Aversion for tragedy explains the passion for escape. When escape is cut off, or when one's lifelong dreams get further and further ahead of one's limitations, the final philosophical issue, as Camus said, is suicide. When we find the myth of the open frontier fraudulent and the reality of our confinement too overwhelming to endure, we understand better why it is that of all the industrialized nations America has the highest rate of suicide. Escape from the closed frontier and its demands takes many forms. Physical suicide is only one way to end anxiety about human finiteness. Another is to falsify the contraries and opposites of human experience and to settle for comfortable but illusory reconciliation. A person who settles for this will usually appeal to authority beyond the walls to relieve the agonizing tensions. But the price paid is to neutralize the polarities of good and evil, the divine and demonic, the light and dark, the thesis and the antithesis—each making independent claims. Neutralizing paradoxes also neutralizes human existence. Destroying the walls eradicates those boundaries in which we identify ourselves as human within this time and this world.

"What we need first and now is to disillusion ourselves," writes Professor Daniel J. Boorstin in *The Image: or What Happened to the American Dream.* "We twentieth-century Americans," he continues, "suffer primarily not from our vices or our weakness, but from our illusions." These are the illusions of youth with its symbolically open frontier, not unlike the youthful fetish for open-mindedness which in reality Professor Allan Bloom suggests, is a condition more often resembling empty-mindedness. Coming of age requires the courage to accept the fact, as Carl Jung said, that we "cannot live the afternoon of life according to the programme of life's morning—for what was great in the morning will be little at evening, and what in the morning was true will at evening become a lie." The condition for coming of age is the tragic vision. Specifically referring to America, Van Wyck Brooks, a literary historian, defined "coming of age" as the process of outgrowing a simplistic view and instead seeing this nation as a "vast Sargasso Sea" containing

all manner of living things . . . phosphorescent gaily coloured, gathered into knots and slotted masses, gelatinous, unformed, flimsy, tangled, rising and falling, floating and merging, here an immense distended belly, there

a tiny rudimentary brain (the gross devouring the fine)—
everywhere an unchecked uncharted, unorganized vitality
like that of the first chaos.

Such a vision cuts through illusions about a past or future
Promised Land and takes us into the awesome depth and
energy and freedom in this brief walled-in existence here and
now. Tragic heroes need not be kings of Greek or Elizabethan
drama; they need be only those persons who, because they are
fully attentive to life's contingencies, know and accept themselves for what they are.[10]

III

The concern here is about the climate of tragedy. That the
open frontier in America offered no such climate needs the
further observation that the closed frontier offers none either,
if by it we mean the ironbound world of the determinists. In
his well-known discussion of the modern temper, naturalist
Joseph Wood Krutch was correct in arguing that the triumph
of determinism means the defeat of tragedy. Krutch erred,
however, in granting the triumph. His central argument in
"The Tragic Fallacy" was that the modern temper regards the
individual as nothing more than a pawn, all actions stripped of
meaning.[11] If such in fact has happened—and who has not
read Aldous Huxley's *Brave New World* and Anthony Burgess'
A Clockwork Orange?—then of course Krutch is right. But the
writer of tragedy declines to accept the end of man; determinism has not triumphed, nor will it so long as man remains the
species he presently is. Tragedies are still to be written, for they
come from within the human spirit, not from the outside
world of the determinist. It is for this reason that the possibilities for tragedy still offer hopeful prospects even within
limitation.

What are the tragedies to be written if the closed frontier
serves as the informing metaphor? Fundamental in such tragedy is not abstract man as mind or spirit but the person of
flesh and bone who is born, suffers and dies. All else said

thereafter comes within the framework of this one fact. Great tragedy accepts this fact and then goes on to tell what happens to the person imprisoned by mortality. It depicts the tragic figure as one who strives to become fully human, to reach out to the limits of selfhood, in order to claim full due as a person. "The only fixed star" in the action of tragedy, says playwright Arthur Miller, is "the need of man to wholly realize himself"[12]—to awaken to the truth of humanity and learn through suffering that to be fully human is to be fully tragic; to discover that suffering, because it is inseparable from tragedy, strengthens man. Such a perspective allows no escape to those realms where Keats' nightingale sings eternally. If for a moment fanciful illusions lift one beyond the walls, suffering brings that person back to the "sole self." One's song is a *miserere* sung in company with all persons who have achieved their full humanity on this side of the wall, the only side where it can be achieved.

With its basic metaphor a closed frontier, tragedy discloses a second condition, namely, the unresolved paradoxes within human life itself. Reason never triumphs here. The Biblical imperative—"Come, let us reason together"—holds little meaning in the world of tragedy where, for example, in Miller's *Death of a Salesman*, Linda stands before the fresh grave of her husband Willy and cries, "I search and search and search, and I can't understand it, Willy. I made the last payment on the house today. Today dear. And there'll be nobody home." The play ends with Linda's final and ironic words: "We're free and clear. We're free. We're free . . . We're free. . . ." In O'Neill's *Long Day's Journey into Night* Edmund claims he once knew what it was like to be free. On a ship bound for Buenos Aires he thought the very sky and sea joined in symbolic union, and he with them. Suddenly for him there was peace, "ecstatic freedom," and meaning. Then the veil fell and he was "lost in the fog again." Whether the image is that of fog, or Van Wyck Brook's Sargasso Sea, or Henry Miller's "air-conditioned nightmare," the straight way is lost amid the ambiguities of existence. Evil and goodness feed on each other; order and chaos fill the same moment. History records humanity's creative and destructive powers, foresight and blindness, freedom and slavery, strength and weakness. Art does the same. Reinhold Niebuhr stresses that we stand "at the juncture of nature and spirit," neither as brute nor angel, neither mere animal nor pure spirit.[13] Our glory comes when we reach the limit of our capacities; at the same time our downfall is assured. Faith is never more human than the believer and thus the tragic tension, "Lord I believe; help thou mine unbelief." Tragedy holds mutually exclusive polarities in tension. Amid conflict tragedy affirms but never resolves this tension, except in death, which still leaves the same old questions for those who live on.

In coming fully to oneself and facing the irreconcilable paradoxes a person must confess what is locked within. But one's tragic sense is not complete without the third element of tragedy which requires touching the bottom of one's own subjectivity, there to find and acknowledge that common birthmark shared by all. The flaw is not in institutions nor in history except as a person is inseparable from them. The flaw of course is what the Greeks called *hubris* and the Christians call sin. Describing this condition Faulkner said that "the heart wants always to be better than it is."[14] Desire is the fatal flaw, and tragedy the freedom to act upon it. The world of tragedy is anthropomorphic. Tragic man, cursed with the desire to make the universe so, seeks to be larger, better, freer, wiser, and in so doing to solve the riddles, to tame the paradoxes, to shape the uncreated conscience of the race. He soars with Icarus and rebels with Prometheus, builds a tower on the plains of Shinar, and strides confidently on an open frontier. Desire is the root of creativity—the desire to leave an enhancing phrase upon the cosmic page. But desire is also the root of destructiveness, and in the fullness of consciousness he must assimilate its tragic consequences.

These three qualities—limitation in fullness, paradox and the flaw—make tragedy possible, just as their discovery marks one's own coming of age. Tragedy and religion: our condition is tragic; our need, religious. In America we see the misplaced emphasis that would have the religious spare us from the tragic. "We remain fixated," says anthropologist Joseph Campbell, "to the unexorcised images of our infancy, and hence disinclined to the necessary passages of our adulthood."[15] Images of infancy take the form of rebirth, as Turner used the term in his frontier hypothesis, or they suggest the happy ending of a fairy tale, the mirthful serenity of old age, or the divine comedy of the soul. These conditions, however, come only after tragedy because their prerequisite is tragedy. Christianity, for example, first serves not as an escape from tragedy but as a mode of entry into it and, therefore, into what it means to be human. Christianity traditionally tells believers about fear and trembling; about peace and the sword; about being forsaken, lost, bewildered, anxious; about having the arrows of God within. This fullness of consciousness is itself a disease, a death, and, therefore, a preparation for faith. But faith is theocentric, and tragedy is anthropomorphic. Faith validates God-talk, but doubt validates the language of tragedy. This is why tragedy never promises salvation, and it forbids reconciliation between faith and doubt.

The tension we know is precisely between our necessity to live in this world and our desire to break through and beyond to a kingdom of permanence and order. The writer of tragedy denies the possibility of this breakthrough, concurring with Camus that Kierkegaard's "leap of faith" is fallacious. In tragedy we cannot "leap" beyond our own place and time. The test is rather the codes by which we live with ourself and others in this world. To Hemingway the code permitted no complaining, no appealing, but complemented affirmation with a sense of limitation and humility. The tragic hero is a life-stylist, always conscious that limitation keeps the human human and that faith, as the extension of desire, brings to full and magnificent flowering the fatal flaw.

IV

Yet some Americans insist the frontier is open and, like novelist William Dean Howells in the 1890s, say that the unpleasant and the tragic find more suitable expression in European literature than in American. It is not suprising that Americans took nearly a hundred years to recognize Melville as a tragic writer. The same applies to Hawthorne and Emily Dickinson. The irony is that Europeans discovered the tragic element in our literature before we ourselves. Whether in this country or elsewhere, tragedy has always been the antithesis of the popular view. Knowing its unsettling, shattering consequences, Plato prescribed that the poet compose nothing contrary to our ideas of law, justice, beauty or goodness. He said a state would be mad to give free license to the tragedian. Still, the Greeks gave the world its greatest tragedies; and, centuries later, despite almost hysterical insistence that Americans continue to stride youthfully on an endless frontier, certain writers have made the tragic journey into the dark forest where the straight way was lost.

Long before Turner made his fateful announcement, Cooper showed that for epical Natty Bumppo the frontier was closed at last, his edenic sanctuary crudely invaded by the rapacious Ishmael Bush. What Hawthorne wrote concerning spiritual malignancy struck even deeper levels of tragedy. As for Melville, his universe consisted of walls, his main effort being to strike through them. His greatest stories, such as *Moby-Dick, Pierre*, "Bartleby the Scrivener," and "The Encantadas," take their structure and meaning from this metaphor. Among writers of this century the tragic vein marks the work of Sherwood Anderson and Ernest Hemingway; Eugene O'Neill, Tennessee Williams, and Arthur Miller; Robert Penn Warren, Flannery O'Connor, and Carson McCullers; John Updike, John Cheever, and Raymond Carver. Most triumphantly it dominates the work of William Faulkner in whose fictional Yoknapatawpha County the smell of honeysuckle, wisteria and verbena still lingers, suggesting the First Garden; but of more formidable consequence stand the courthouse and the jail, one testifying to man's rational madness, the other to his tragic gall and travail.

Among several nineteenth- and twentieth-century American writers whose works specifically illustrate the tragedy of the closed frontier, three novelists in particular afford valuable study. With Mark Twain, Ole Rölvaag and Nathanael West, the American frontier dream clashes with the tragedy of those people who acted upon this dream. What emerges testifies to the fact that as fundamental as the frontier was to the national experience, so too was the tragedy.

6

Adventures of Huckleberry Finn

BARRIERS AND BOUNDARIES

W HATEVER THE DIFFICULTIES in defining trag-
edy—either as a literary mode or as a way of looking at life—
readers of *Huckleberry Finn* have been wary of calling this
American classic a tragedy. Why this should be the case may be
inherent in the novel itself, or it may be that Americans in
general are reluctant to see anything American as tragic. Un-
questionably the nineteenth century gave us a great literary
tragedy in *Moby-Dick*, and there may be no debate that
Melville's next novel, *Pierre*, or Hawthorne's *Scarlet Letter* de-
serve similar judgment. But to many readers Mark Twain's
masterpiece has seemed in some way too shapeless for tragedy,
too lacking in height or depth, too humorous; and Huck Finn,
on both land and river, too elusive to call a tragic hero.

Reluctance to see Twain's novel as tragedy leads to some
interesting speculation nevertheless. Henry Nash Smith, for
example, notes (italics mine) that "what had begun as a comic
story developed *incipiently* tragic implications contradicting
the premises of comedy." Time and again Professor Smith
comes close to his own premise of tragedy, then draws back.
He says that whereas the "vernacular persona is an essentially
comic figure, the character in Huck's meditation is potentially
tragic." He observes in Huck "a melancholy *if not exactly* tragic
strain," yet notes with qualification that what Twain had on
his hands in the last part of the novel was "a hybrid—a comic
story in which the protagonists have acquired *something like*
tragic depth." All the business on the Phelps plantation Professor Smith regards as a "maneuver by which Mark Twain

beats his way back from *incipient* tragedy to the comic resolution called for by the original conception of the story."[1]

This same critical ambivalence characterizes what many
other readers have discovered about the novel. They reach far
enough to find the conditions for tragedy; they may use the
terms "tragic" or "tragedy," but they also back away, leaving
undeveloped what they have implied. T. S. Eliot suggests
"there is no more solitary character in fiction," comparing
Huck with Ulysses, Faust, Don Quixote, Don Juan and Ham-
let. Yet, says Eliot, Huck is no tragic figure; a tragic ending to
the novel "would reduce [Huck] to the level of those whom
we pity." Literary critics like Richard Chase agree that a tragic
conclusion would be inappropriate for Huck, though Chase
points out not only that Huck's world is a pattern of "con-
tentment and horror" but that Huck himself knows "the real
world with a tragic awareness." James M. Cox argues that
Huck's initiation into society carries with it both "tragic
irony" and Huck's own "inner awareness" that such member-
ship will destroy his character and deny his values. On the
other hand, this awareness is what William C. Spengemann
suggests is lacking; nevertheless, in juxtaposing the ideal and
the real, innocence and evil, the book contains, he says, "the
stuff of tragedy." Still another example of critical ambivalence
comes in W. R. Moses' assertion that in many respects Huck's
voyage resembles Dante's in the *Inferno*: Huck is "involved in
evil, fights against it and suffers under it as a hero should and
must." "Yet," says Moses, "he is a *boy*," and "it would *not* be
appropriate for the American waif to bear the ultimate burden
of the tragic hero."[2]

These few examples serve to point out the difficulties in
one's claiming that *Huckleberry Finn* is an American tragedy. It
can be more easily argued that Mark Twain himself was a
tragic figure and let biography carry the burden of tragedy in
the novel. In *The Ordeal of Mark Twain*, Van Wyck Brooks has
given an unforgettable picture of Twain's tortured conscience,
a picture that takes on more crushing impact in Justin Kaplan's
biography, *Mr. Clemens and Mark Twain*. To read Kaplan's

last three chapters—"Get me out of business!" "Never quite sane in the night" and "Whited sepulchre"—is to encounter a truly dark, divided and tragic human being. It is curious, therefore, that some readers who hold back their judgment about *Huckleberry Finn* as tragedy justify their restraint by suggesting that Mark Twain was afraid to write tragedy—or, more precisely, that he was reluctant to develop the tragic implications that stole into what he intended to be a comic story. He had to beat his way back, says Professor Smith, to avoid being engulfed by complexities far beyond his original plan.

We know Twain took seven years to write this book. We know from Walter Blair's study that even though Twain's public success and affluence steadily increased during this period, he was plagued by personal misfortunes, literary failures, the Whittier birthday fiasco and, most importantly, by his disillusionment with nothing less than humanity itself.[3] We can only guess the psychological unrest tormenting Twain at this time, perhaps best seen in *The Prince and the Pauper*, written between 1877 and 1881, approximately midway between the start and finish of Huckleberry Finn. But to accept Leo Marx's claim that Huck's quest never brought him to a full tragic vision because Twain himself suffered "failure of nerve"[4] is not only to bind the novel irrevocably to the author's biography but also to gloss over the novel's tragic elements. It may be that Twain could not help himself. Once he had created Huck and developed his complex and many-layered inner life, Twain found the tragic fact that Huck, in order to survive in society, had to repress his anxieties and live on Tom Sawyer surfaces. When through a mistake Aunt Sally Phelps gives Tom's name to Huck, the central irony emerges: "It was like being born again," says Huck, "I was so glad to find out who I was." The novel's whole last section, from chapter 32 on, is a dramatic travesty of this rebirth, of Huck's becoming Tom. The tragedy rests in the irony that only as Tom can Huck survive. As Tom, Huck has the necessary armor of untruth to safeguard his vulnerable self within. When his identity is at last revealed in chapter 42, Huck as Huck can no longer stay around. Twain, therefore, calls the next (and last) chapter, "Nothing More to Write." For Huck to be adopted and civilized by Aunt Sally means the death of something within himself.

II

The travesty of rebirth is part of a sequence that portrays Huck as a double. One side of his nature is rebellious, intuitive, spontaneous; the other side is logical and fully acculturated. These two sides manifest their equivalents in two kinds of conscience, one constantly troubled by human problems, the other troubled by abstract, impersonal ones. One side is the real Me; the other side the social Me, or what Emerson called the Not Me. The point is that both sides are very much real, both are in conflict with each other; and if reconciliation between the two occurs, it will be the former that yields.

We see Huck as a Tom figure at the beginning of the novel. As early as the second paragraph we learn that his effort to rebel against Widow Douglas and her civilizing ways has been only short-lived: that although he "lit out" Tom has persuaded him to return on the condition that if he "would go back to the widow and be respectable," he would be allowed to join the band of robbers. "So I went back," Huck confesses. His commitment to Tom's code spells his death as Huck. For the code, written by Tom and sworn to by all members of the band, demands total allegiance regardless of the duties exacted and foretells the dreadful consequences should those duties not be followed. The oath

swore every boy to stick to the band, and never tell any of the secrets; and if anybody done anything to any boy in the band, whichever boy was ordered to kill that person and his family must do it, and he mustn't eat and he mustn't sleep till he had killed them and hacked a cross in their breasts, which was the sign of the band. And nobody that didn't belong to the band could use that mark, and if he did he must be sued; and if he done it again he must be killed. And if anybody that belonged to the band told the secrets, he must have his throat cut, and then have his carcass burnt up and the ashes scattered all around, and his name blotted off the list with blood and never mentioned again by the gang, but have a curse put on it and be forgot forever.

It was to this oath—which resembles something as old as the medieval church's curse of excommunication and as modern as fascism, the KKK and 1984—that Huck pledged himself in blood. "I made my mark on the paper," he again confesses, not unlike Melville's Ishmael, who, pledging total commitment to Ahab and the crew, admitted, "my shouts had gone up with the rest; my oath had been welded with theirs."

We begin to see Huck's other side after he kills himself as a Tom figure. Up to the time he fakes his own murder to escape Pap (chapter 7), he conforms reasonably well to society's expectations. At first he hated school, but "by and by I got so I could stand it." He says that the longer he went to school "the easier it got to be." He admits he "was getting sort of used to the widow's ways," and the widow thought he was "doing very satisfactory." And even when Pap forces him away, holding him prisoner in the shack, Huck admits that "it warn't long after that till I was used to being where I was, and liked it—all but the cowhide part." But depicting Pap not only as the worst kind of social racist but also as a victim of delirium tremens gave Twain the opportunity to justify Huck's fake ax-killing. The sigificance of this death, however, is not that it allows Huck, as a Tom figure, to escape from Pap, but that it frees Huck to become Huck. What he earlier killed of himself when he swore allegiance to Tom can now be reborn.

It must be made clear that this rebirth, a process in the novel extending roughly from chapter 8 to chapter 31, is radically different from the one described in chapter 32, titled "I Have a New Name." Being born again as Tom Sawyer, in chapter 32, was "easy and comfortable." It made him feel "pretty comfortable all down one side," but the fact that it also made him feel "pretty uncomfortable all up the other" reminds us that in the preceding chapter Huck had finally arrived at his unequivocal fullness as Huck, an experience leaving him *un*easy and *un*comfortable, to say the least. From chapter 8 on, Huck Finn, as a double, struggles with his own death angel no less than did Pap, and his freedom from it in chapter 31 marks him as a tragic hero who for a moment stands triumphant over social and moral entaglements but who, too soon, will again be imprisoned by them.

This emergence of Huck as a radically reconstituted personality—as one authentically reborn—begins only after he has committed himself not to a code but to a person. This commitment to Jim and to his safety ironically frees Huck to find and to know himself. Thus Nigger Jim is the means of Huck's deliverance, much as the pagan Queequeg is of Ishmael's. Huck and Jim are both refugees from society; both wish for the freedom they romantically associate with nature, specifically the river. On Jackson Island they come together, finding in each other the goodness and love that social codes had stifled. "I warn't lonesome now," says Huck, who, after hearing about Jim's escape, pledges to Miss Watson's runaway slave, "I ain't a-going to tell." This oath in chapter 8 marks the beginning of Huck's moral struggle, for by welding himself to Jim he calls into question all those social values that had kept them apart.

On the novel's deepest level Huck's brooding misgivings, striking dread into his heart and repeatedly leaving him "in a sweat," come from the freedom he gains when he chooses to love persons rather than follow people. In choosing to give his highest allegiance to Jim, a member of no respectable band, he ironically gains freedom within the hell to which respectability consigns him. Huck's real freedom is not on the raft, idyllic as that frontier life seems. His only real freedom comes when he squarely faces a decision within Tom's world and accepts the curse of excommunication that world decrees.

The turmoil taking place in Huck's inner world, like the trauma of birth itself, has its parallel in the vast exterior world. The great artistry of Mark Twain appears in this perfect blend of what Huck sees on the outside and what he feels within. The first clues to this inner condition are supplied by the frightful omens haunting both Huck and Jim. Throughout the early chapters certain portents terrify one or the other: spiders, witches, talk of a floating corpse, Pap's foot tracks in the snow, a hair ball, young birds "flying a yard or two at a time and lighting," storms, handling a snakeskin. About such occurrences Huck asks Jim if there were not any good signs. "Mighty few—an' *dey* ain't no use to a body," he answers.

This tone of foreboding becomes more intense during action that takes place on the river. Many readers have thought the contrary: that the river represents an idyllic retreat, a place of perfect freedom and naturalness. Extending this notion further, critic Philip Young thinks that the river symbolizes "a dark and silent unknown," and that what characterizes Huck's several departures from the land to the river are the qualities of "ease, silence, and darkness."[5] But as Huck's inner world of troubled conscience cannot thus be fully described, neither can the river, the scene again and again of horror, violence, and intrigue—with, for example, the house of death floating by, the killers on board the *Walter Scott*, fog and the separation of Huck and Jim, the steamboat that runs them down, slave hunters, the Duke and the Dauphin, and violent storms. With proper understatement Huck observes that "the raft was a most uncommon lively place."

But it is on the land where Huck's boiling conscience—the conscience concerned with persons rather than abstractions— finds its most telling correlatives. For Mark Twain this was clearly to be the payoff. If he were to delineate Huck as a tragic character—one whose real self must confront the equally real world he lives in—Twain would have to show the boy the worst of his own society, including all those corrupt values that molded him into the boy he culturally was. The tension inherent in Huck's tragic position had to be pulled taut, and whether Twain's reluctance to do this accounted for his putting the manuscript aside after a summer's work of 400 pages in 1876 remains unknown. Upon the completion of *Tom Sawyer* the previous year, he had written to William Dean Howells that he (Twain) had decided not to "take the chap [Tom] beyond boyhood," for "if I went on now and took him into manhood, he would just lie like all the one-horse men in literature and the reader would conceive a hearty contempt for him." "By and by," he continued, "I shall take a boy of twelve and run him on through life (in the first person) but not Tom Sawyer—he would not be a good character for it."[6] To Huck was given the burden of experience that brought him figuratively into manhood and literally into tragic understanding. It was with chapter 17 that Twain resumed the novel, adding to it the kind of scathing realism and dark power that puts into sharp relief what Huck is morally in for now that he has pledged himself to Jim. In chapter 15 that pledge had become totally significant when Huck humbly apologized for tricking Jim into thinking that their separation in the fog was only Jim's dream. This apology is important evidence of growth in moral insight. Chapter 16 then brings Huck face to face with the hard fact that he is actually helping a slave escape. "My conscience got to stirring me up hotter than ever," Huck says. "I was . . . all in a sweat to tell on him. . . . I just felt sick. But I says, I *got* to do it—I can't get *out* of it." By the time Twain finished this chapter and put the manuscript aside, the pattern of the novel was clearly drawn; he had only to summon the courage and to perfect the artistry in order to follow where the novel's tragic design pointed. He did both.

III

There is no need to recount all the shattering experiences Huck underwent each time he stepped off his raft. That he wanted to regard them merely as adventures, after the manner of Tom, suggests an understandable desire to remain detached and therefore unscarred. In carrying out his own fake murder, for example, he said, "I did wish Tom Sawyer was there; I knowed he would take an interest in this kind of business, and throw in the fancy touches." In later boasting to Jim about this same business, he could not resist the observation that "Tom Sawyer couldn't get up no better plan than what I had done." And in persuading an apprehensive Jim to search the wrecked steamboat with him, Huck asked, "Do you reckon Tom Sawyer would ever go by this thing? Not for a pie, he wouldn't. He'd call it an adventure." But what start as adventures to Huck soon become searing realities. He sees the cruelty of river townsmen; the pathos of broken slave families; the deceit of confidence men, fakers, itinerant evangelists, obscene show-men, masquerading all the while as noblemen; the hypocrisy and vicious feuding of the aristocracy; the bullying of a mur-derer and the cowardice of a lynch mob; and, woven through-out these episodes, the ever-present reminder of ghosts, corpses, evil omens and murder. "It was enough to make a body ashamed of the human race," Huck says at one point. "I never see anything so disgusting . . . it was just sickening," he says another time. Or: "Well, it made me sick to see it. . . . It was a dreadful thing to see." What he saw was the damned human race, and what he felt was the soul sickness of one exposed to the fraudulent social basis of his own professed faith.

Matching the courage to run Huck "on through life" was the artistic technique by which Twain sent Huck on this dreadful journey. This technique is marked by the multiple names, disguises and concealments given to Huck. Paradoxical is that in order to survive in society Huck must wear masks even though masks alone do not insure his survival. It is true that without disguises Huck would be unable to live as Huck. It is equally true that the one disguise he could never effect— the one lie he could never pray—was to regard Jim as only another mask. Sometimes Huck is Tom; he is also Sarah Williams, George Peters, George Jackson, and hilariously enough, "Sarah Mary Williams George Elexander Peters." Tom is William Thompson and Sid; the two rapscallions are the Duke of Bridgewater and "Looy the Seventeen," later Harvey Wilkes and his brother William; Jim is King Lear as well as a "Sick Arab." All these disguises and more suggest a world of masks and games, swindlers and con men, pedigrees and Prufrocks—in short, a chaotic world in which the true and false are indistinguishable except to Huck, who perceives re-alities within the chaos and who, unmasked, answers when

Jim calls him "honey." It is this name, and Huck's precarious freedom to respond to it, that means his survival as Huck.

To suggest this crazy fabric of societal life, Mark Twain supplies more than disguises, hoaxes, schemes and pseudonyms. As technique, nothing is more fundamental to the novel than its irony—an irony by which Twain takes his readers to the heart of tragedy. From the title itself we get our earliest clue; we learn, as mentioned before, that Huck's "adventures" were experiences of the most shattering intensity. Tom has no understanding of this fact. When the two boys meet on the Phelps farm, Tom wants to know "all about" what had befallen Huck because to Tom "it was a grand adventure, and mysterious, and so it hit him where he lived." "But," Huck says to him, "leave it alone till by and by," knowing that the real "adventures" of Huckleberry Finn he could never share.

Irony deepens as Huck and Jim escape to the river. This is not the same Mississippi River Twain wrote about in the seven sketches of 1875 for the *Atlantic Monthly* and published the same year as *Old Times on the Mississippi*. In that earlier book the river is an object external to Twain, age forty. Even though he describes it affectionately and acknowledges its "eluding and ungraspable" quality, the river is still outside his creative imagination, still either the river of traditionally romantic associations or else the river where he once learned to pilot a steamboat. Perhaps one can argue that *Old Times on the Mississippi* does symbolically describe a rite of initiation into the river's dangerous and intricate ways. Yet, the powerful, tragic overtones are clearly absent, nor are they found in the enlarged 1882 version, *Life on the Mississippi*, a book Twain intended as little more than a travelogue. That volume elicited from him a few days after he finished it the fierce comment: "I will not interest myself in anything connected with the wretched Goddamned book."[7] No, the Mississippi River that Mark Twain imaginatively created for his masterpiece is clearly a different river from that found in the earlier two books.

The river Huck and Jim flee to holds mythic terrors as profound as the superstition-ridden psychic depths of its travelers. At night its fateful currents take Jim beyond Cairo, where he was to have found freedom, and into ever more hostile country where, eventually, he will be turned in by the king "for forty dirty dollars." Where the river will take Huck is implied in the last scene Twain wrote before he put the manuscript away. Coming upstream was a steamboat, pounding ever closer in the darkness, its form looming like "a black cloud with rows of glow-worms around it; but all of a sudden she bulged out, big and scary with a long row of wide-open furnace doors shining like red-hot teeth." As the fiery monster smashed through the raft, Huck dived into the black water, his escape serving ironically as a ritual of baptism. "I aimed," he said, "to find the bottom," an ominous indication of what awaits him.

All the terrors and nightmares of hell evoked by the river are not to be forgotten even when, at the beginning of chapter 19, we come to a description many readers, including Ernest Hemingway, have justifiably regarded as one of the most beautifully lyrical paeans Mark Twain ever wrote about the river.[8] Demonic blackness has now become an ethereal radiance as the dawn spreads its gentle light over the Mississippi, from whose banks blows a breeze "so cool and fresh and sweet to smell on account of the woods and flowers." It could almost be the river Ganges, the water as sacramental as Walden Pond, the morning as beatific as when Billy Budd met the dawn of his transfiguration. There is now no desperate plunge into the water's depths; instead, Huck and Jim "slid into the river and had a swim, so as to freshen up and cool off," and then "set down on the sandy bottom where the water was about knee-deep, and watched the day-light come."

The river is both benign and treacherous, and it is this conflict between the two that gives ironic density to the novel, not wholly unlike the irony of Melville's masterpiece in which we learn that the most dreaded creatures of the sea glide hidden beneath the loveliest surface tints of blue. Each aspect of the river must be recognized, especially what T. S. Eliot called in the *Four Quartets* "implacable," that quality serving as a "reminder of / What men choose to forget."

The same irony is found in Huck's apparent simpleness and freedom. But Huck is neither simple nor free, and his innocence has a dark side much like the river. If the inscrutable Pap is the one who puts Huck in touch with the deeper human forces, it is Jim who tells Huck about these forces within Pap and, most importantly, within Huck himself. Jim does this through a crucial prophecy he interprets from the hair ball in chapter 4. The prophecy tells about two angels hovering around Pap, one white and the other black. "De white one gits him to go right a little while, den de black one sail in en bust it all up. . . . A body can't tell yit which one gwyne to fetch him at de las'." As for Huck, Jim continues:

> You gwyne to have considable trouble in yo' life, en considable joy. Sometimes you gwyne to git hurt, en sometimes you gwyne to git sick; but every time you's gwyne to git well ag'in. Dey's two gals flyin' 'bout you in yo' life. One uv 'em's light en t'other one is dark. One is rich en t'other is po'. You's gwyne to marry de po' one fust en de rich one by en by. You wants to keep 'way fum de water as much as you kin, en don't run no resk, 'kase it's down in de bills dat you's gwyne to get hung.

The prophecy not only warns what will befall Huck but makes as explicit as any other statement in the novel the ironic nature of both Huck and the river. If innocence and benign naturalness were all there was to be found, then the whole possibility of tragedy would disappear. But Twain's view of life is tragic, which means that life is synonymous with conflict, just as conflict is the essence of irony. Perhaps irony overreaches itself when Twain has tragic insights come to a seemingly innocent boy whose awareness can hardly be expected to encompass the full meaning of tragedy. This argument, however, fails to take into account the myth of the American Adam who represents reborn innocence. This is the myth Twain emphatically destroys in the novel. Huck's painful rebirth, which culminates in chapter 31, does not deliver him from a world of complexity and finiteness but instead thrusts him squarely into it. His is the loss of innocence, not the

American Adam's recovery of it. His is the decision to be a man, not the Adamic freedom to remain a child. To Huck comes the tragic, unWordsworthian realization that the man *is* the father of the child.

IV

At the heart of the novel is the question of freedom, though not the kind of freedom readers have commonly associated with Huck's flight to the river. The central metaphor is neither the river, the land, nor all those ploys connected with the metaphor of disguise. With profound irony the theme of freedom comes through the metaphor of prison, the equivalent of a closed frontier. Thus we see that Jim the slave is the freest of men; whereas Tom, the perfect representative of what society calls freedom, is bound by the invisible chains of custom and tradition. Neither Jim nor Tom "sweat" over their identity. One knows he is a slave and thereby possesses that secret if unconscious wisdom of his own freedom. The other knows he is free and thereby lives deluded as to his real enslavement. Jim is Jim and Tom is Tom, their occasional disguises causing them no anxiety, their respective conditions of freedom and imprisonment leading to no conscious ambivalence. The tragic figure is Huck who knows both the freedom of conscience and the bondage of convention, who lives through the terrible cycles of death and rebirth and death again, who at the end of the novel learns he has won $6000 but lost a father, and who still fatefully seeks the freedom of some illusory open frontier. This after he has experienced the only freedom he will ever know—the freedom within what Melville called "a joint stock company of two": Ishmael and Queequeg bound together; Huck and Jim, free to love only within the strictures of their society.

Huck achieves freedom within this social framework, not outside or beyond it. This freedom has meaning only as it is inseparable from his condition as a child of culture. Huck's famous declaration of independence in chapter 31 paradoxically occurs at that moment when his individuality—won at so great a struggle—merges with that of Jim. At such a moment in *Moby-Dick* Ishmael's free will was dealt "a mortal wound." So too was Huck's, and the same tragic irony is in Huck's cry, "All right, then, I'll go to hell," the hell of social disgrace in which the grace of love can flourish.

This then is Huck's true rebirth, one of the great moments in American literature. But what then of the last twelve chapters? Does the unity of the work break down when Tom comes into the foreground to engineer Jim's elaborate escape? Are these chapters Mark Twain's comic way of avoiding the tragic?

With prison as the novel's key metaphor—plus all the imagery, situations and meanings associated with it in the novel—these last twelve chapters are indispensable to Twain's tragic meaning. That we are prepared for his use of this metaphor long before it dominates the last third of the book is important, for we see it as an extension and enlargement of earlier situations. Miss Watson hems in Huck with endless restrictions: "Don't put your feet up there, Huckleberry"; "Don't scrunch up like that, Huckleberry"; "Don't gap and stretch like that, Huckleberry." Illustrations abound to show Huck's freedom tightly limited by his social context and historical heritage. In this connection Huck's clothes aptly symbolize this bondage, for whenever he could he went naked, "day and night," the new clothes the Grangerfords made for him being "too good to be comfortable." Of course Huck was also physically imprisoned by Pap. And in a sense, he was entangled by all those undelineated forces in his psychic life, not only by the vast web of superstitions but also by dreams of violence and murder that, he said, "I ain't ever going to get shut of." As for Jim, the institution of slavery made certain what his limitations were. Both Huck and Jim are prisoners, each tells the other of his escape when the two first meet on Jackson Island, and throughout their odyssey the constant need to escape one tight squeeze after another serves to emphasize their confinement. The freedom to be himself that Huck achieves in chapter 31 echoes Melville's reminder in *Mardi* that "Freedom is the name for a thing that is *not* freedom." Huck's freedom is meaningful only through the tragic fact that he remains a prisoner of his culture, a fact about which the novel's last twelve chapters leave no doubt.

In the first of these last chapters Huck has only to set foot on the Phelps plantation to wish he were dead and "done with it all." His wish is soon granted when Aunt Sally calls him Tom. As Huck, he has known self-reliance; but this condition leaves him too exposed, too free, and he therefore must die in order to be reborn as Tom, symbolic of his necessary and inevitable reentering the prison house of Tom's world. Huck's willingness to obey Tom's "Dark, Deep-laid Plans" in chapter 35 recalls his swearing to Tom's "dark oath" in chapter 2. In both instances he resigns himself to the rules Tom twines around him.

Huck's own plans to steal Jim from the custody of Silas Phelps are simple and straightforward, but for this reason they have no place among the belittered difficulties Tom invents. The finality of Tom's ways squeezes unequivocally upon Huck. Tom says, "It don't make no difference how foolish it is, it's the *right* way—and it's the regular way. And there ain't no *other* way, that ever *I* heard of, and I've read all the books that gives any information about these things." Tom's intricate strategy is matched only by the tools he demands for the job: candles and candlesticks, a sheet, a spoon, a shirt, case-knives, a rope ladder, shovels, an undecipherable coat of arms, inscriptions for Jim to write on a rock, a grindstone, rattlesnakes for Jim to tame, rats and spiders, a warming pan, a "witch-pie," a flower for Jim to water with his tears, "nonnamous letters" and so on. Within this fantastic network Tom himself is in high spirits. Huck observes "it was the best fun" Tom ever had in his life, and "the most intellectural," Tom wanting nothing more than to "keep it up all the rest of our lives and leave Jim to our children to get out."

As for Jim, Huck knows "he couldn't see no sense in the most of it, but he allowed we was white folks and knowed better than him; so he was satisfied, and said he would do it all just as Tom said." Tom's game leaves Jim's deeper self untouched. With complete acceptance Jim remarks, "I never knowed b'fo' twas so much bother and trouble to be a prisoner." Tom's news that Miss Watson had set Jim free in her will two months earlier only corroborates what Jim's real condition has been throughout the novel. He has been free all along in the sense that his sorrow, compassion, joy and love sprang genuinely and unambiguously from his individual humanity. Tom, on the other hand, is so entrapped by his own game that he allows for no expression of feelings that might identify his humanity with someone else's. The chilling horror of this fact is not only that Tom, when wounded by a bullet, remains insensitive to the love behind Jim's all-night ministrations, but that to Tom, life itself is nothing more than a game in which rules take precedence over persons. Jim's plight is never anything but an abstraction to Tom. All the stratagems for freeing Jim actually keep the two apart. The icy impersonality required by the game is best seen when Tom explains why he supervised Jim's escape, all the while knowing that Miss Watson had freed him. "Why," he said, "I wanted the *adventure* of it; and I'd 'a' waded neck-deep in blood to—[have it?]."

Where is Huck within the maze of these last chapters? He takes his stance between the person of Jim and the persona of Tom, between the assertive and personal forces from within and the inhibiting, impersonal forces from without, between individual freedom and social rule. His is a tragic stance requiring that he compromise with what Henry Adams called the "perplexing, warring, irreconcilable problems, irreducible opposites." "From earliest childhood," Adams wrote in his *Education*, he "was accustomed to feel that, for him, life was double." The same insight comes to Huck who, as a double, discovers that only by killing something within himself can he live in this world. His resolution is never static. Appalled by Tom's sense of adventure as a mere game, Huck is also a little beguiled by it. Embracing the individuality of Jim, he still feels the hard truth Melville's Babbalanja voiced: "to be, is to be something." The "something" Jim was, was a black, a slave, a socially consigned inferior. Unlike Melville's Pierre, who learned "that unless he committed a sort of suicide as to the practical things of this world, he never can hope to regulate his earthly conduct by that same heavenly soul," Huck Finn learns the contrary. Unless he kills something of his soul, he can never live amid the practical things of this world. To Huck there are no cosmic sanctions, no metaphysics, no "strange brown god," no Aristotle, Hegel or Wordsworth to posit unity and wholeness. Even more significantly, there is no Whitman, no American Dream, no open frontier. There is only the world he lives in but never made.

What makes this novel important in the development of American tragedy is that we see for the first time the meaning of America's closed frontier. Huck's journey does not take him to the stars but only into the hell of his own civilization, from which there is no safety valve of escape. At this point of no exit we see the fierce collision between what the American Dream promised and what the inexorable limitations of the closed frontier set down. Spiritual deliverance collided with moral finiteness; or, more to the point in Twain's novel, democratic ideals of selfhood collided with social realities. The frontier spirit represented by the pioneer's singular courage and enterprise had resulted in the builder being imprisoned by the edifice he built. All that is left in such a prison is one's own personality. Philosopher Karl Jaspers suggests that "in acting out" one's personality, in realizing one's selfhood "even unto death," one finds his only deliverance.[9] For a crucial moment Huck found this deliverance, this new birth; but what makes his existence tragic is that, as critic Northrop Frye says, "every new birth provokes the return of an avenging death. . . . On one side of the tragic hero is an opportunity for freedom, on the other the inevitable consequence of losing that freedom."[10] So it is with Huck Finn. To him the lesson of tragedy taught possibility as well as limitation.

This irony touches the last two sentences of the novel. For Huck the possibility still exists "to light out for the territory ahead of the rest." In this Indian Territory (later Oklahoma), Huck hopes to rediscover that moment of deliverance like the one he experienced with Jim. His fate is to hope he can stay "ahead of the rest." Though he once found his freedom among them, he continues to search for it beyond. A final and cryptic postscript to this tragic fate comes in the brief entry Twain wrote in his notebook in 1891 (contemplating an extension of the Tom-Huck story): "Huck comes back sixty years old, from nobody knows where—and crazy."[11]

7

Ole Rölvaag and the Immigrant Promise Denied

IN *Their Fathers' God*, the third volume of Ole Rölvaag's trilogy of the American prairie, Peder Holm asks Nikoline Johansen, "What is *hilder* like?" Newly arrived from Norway and soon to return, Nikoline explains to American-born Peder that *hilder* is a mirror-like mirage appearing in the sky on certain Norwegian summer nights when the air is "clear and warm and still." The islands off the northern coast

> stand on their heads in the air—they just float there. The ships sail with their masts pointing down; up in the sky you understand. Oh, you can't imagine how beautiful such nights are! . . . It's a fairyland and you aren't a bit afraid. . . . All space is a magic mirror . . . you see only phantasms floating in a great stillness . . . you don't dare breathe for fear they'll pass away [ellipses Rölvaag's].

When Peder says that life in America is a *hilder*, Nikoline distinguishes between the American and the Norwegian: "We know when we see *hilder*," she said; "we can tell it and make allowance. You Americans believe all you see until you run your heads against a stone wall; then you don't believe anything any more." "You're an American," she added, "you saw *hilder* and believed it."[1]

Fundamental to the American experience are these illusions, these often vague but nonetheless compelling dreams that beckoned the immigrant and the pioneer to build a kingdom or, at best, to make his house a castle. From these same dreams came the inevitable tragedy, most dramatically symbolized by the closed frontier. Inherent in the American experience is tragedy that even yet has not been understood. With every dream of freedom there is the conflicting reality of limitation; with every absolute—be it equality, justice, human dignity—there is tragic contradiction. Among the greatest idealists of American literature a slender thread of tragedy appears. Even Emerson found his philosophical scheme incomplete until he had written "Experience" and "Fate," and had lived in what he called "the house of pain." Among the less great—especially among those who make public pronouncements intended for the popular mind—the absence of this tragic thread indicates ignorance of the American experience rather than optimism about it. As for the Norwegian-born Ole Edvart Rölvaag, his writing combines the themes of both freedom and fate, society and solitude, and the awesome price of kingdom building. What his fictional trilogy—*Giants in the Earth* (1927), *Peder Victorious* (1929) and *Their Fathers' God* (1931)—makes clear is that to see *hilder* and believe it is to learn the lesson of American tragedy.

By the time Rölvaag joined the faculty at St. Olaf College in Northfield, Minnesota, in 1906, ten years after he first arrived in this country as a twenty-year-old immigrant, he was persuaded that two powerful forces had shaped American life. These were Immigration and the Westward Movement. He could number himself part of the first, writing in his journal on July 29, 1896: "It is done; it is done. I have left home."[2] Only imaginatively could he count himself a western pioneer, though doing so was not difficult in Elk Point, South Dakota, where he arrived in September and immediately experienced prairie life as monotonous and without depth and nuances. Yet as he went on to earn his diploma (with honors) from Augustana Academy in Canton in 1901 and his bachelor's degree four years later from St. Olaf College, he began to see something epical in both Immigration and the Westward Movement. To Rölvaag the immigrants in the 1840s and after resembled Vikings, acting out their part in a great national epic. Though he mainly testified for the Norwegian immigrants, Rölvaag interpreted this entire movement west as the expression of purposeful and heroic idealism, as singleness of will. Addressing students in 1907 he said that such singleness of will, if it is to remain total, must aim at "the good," and, finally, it must be brought into harmony with the singleness of God's will.[3] It was in this way that Rölvaag challenged his youthful students and conceived his own purpose. In greater perspective, he applied the same ideas to the American frontier experience. Writing some twenty years later of it, he said that the pioneers "threw themselves blindly into the Impossible and accomplished the Unbelievable. . . . Not since the day man first took up his struggles has the human race known such faith and a like confidence—once more the race had been made young!"[4]

Such idealism colors Rölvaag's teaching and public addresses. On deeper and more creative levels, however, his imagery of pioneers as Israelites and of the West as Canaan gives way to an Ibsen-like gloom and a hovering sense of fatality. The central problem Rölvaag faced was whether to write an American epic or an American tragedy. Through the character of Per Hansa in *Giants in the Earth* Rölvaag had created an epical Moses figure. Per Hansa had led his family across the wilderness; at Spring Creek he had founded a Norwegian settlement that to him was a kingdom, and he had envisioned his own grand estate—his royal mansion, magnificent barn and endless fields of golden wheat. "The palace itself would be white, with green cornices . . . the big barn would be as red as blood, with cornices of driven snow."[5] Per Hansa's "divine restlessness" would keep him forever striding forward "with outstretched arms toward the future." Little matter that on the verge of fulfillment he would die, like Moses; for like the great patriarch, Per Hansa would have a successor, his own son, Peder Victorious, who, in the last novel of the trilogy, will echo his father: "Our task is here to build up happiness so great and so wonderful that the glory of it will brighten up the far corners of the world."

Had Rölvaag chosen to write his trilogy as epic, he would have had to portray action commensurate with the idealism engendered by the myth of the West. This of course he did in the character of Per Hansa, but he dies a third of the way through the trilogy. Furthermore, the reader begins to suspect only halfway through the first book that Per Hansa, despite his stature as a western hero, will not triumph, and, in fact, the forces of fate will verify only too clearly Pascal's observation in *Pensées* that "man is but a reed, the feeblest thing in Nature."

The chapter titles concluding the first book are ominous enough: "Facing the Great Desolation," "The Heart That Dared Not Let in the Sun," "On the Border of Utter Darkness," "The Power of Evil in High Places," and, finally, "The Great Plain Drinks the Blood of Christian Men and Is Satisfied." Within these chapters Rölvaag allows no sentimentality to mitigate the woe and desperation visited upon the pioneers. One evening, for example, after a three-day fog had finally lifted and the western sun was transforming the clouds into "marvellous fairy castles," Per Hansa's wife, Beret, sat watching a lone wagon slowly moving over the prairie from the northeast. She and Per Hansa were soon to discover that inside the wagon, which was bearing a pitiable family of four, the mother crouched with her wrists bound with strong rope to the handles of a large immigrant chest; so insane with grief was she after burying her small son behind on the prairie that Jakob, her husband, could restrain her delirium only with rope. To Per Hansa the woman looked as if she had been "crucified." In telling his story Jakob could say little more than "Fate just willed it so. . . . It isn't any use to fight against Fate."

Although Per Hansa, his progeny, and his fellow pioneers will physically master the wilderness, as Frederick Jackson Turner described the pioneers' eventual triumph, other incidents in these final chapters of *Giants* suggest that more powerful forces are at work than those with which the Norwegian, as epic hero, can cope. Physical desolation caused by locusts season after season leaves Per Hansa outraged and bewildered, not only because the crops were ruined but because he found it impossible to outguess the deadly insects. "No creatures ever acted so whimsically or showed such a lack of rational, orderly method. They might entirely lay waste to one field, while they ate only a few rods into the next; a third, lying close beside the others, they might not choose to touch at all." Even more baffling to Per Hansa is Beret's oncoming breakdown. He can do nothing to assuage her feelings of psychological desolation, loneliness, exile; her certainty that an inexorable destiny possesses her life; her guilt for having conceived Peder out of wedlock; her anguish as she secretly prepares the family chest for her own coffin, in which Per Hansa later finds her still breathing but tightly coiled like a fetus. The most mysterious force is death itself, ironically claiming Per Hansa on the same winter day that he thinks about the barn he would build next fall—"a real show barn," he calls it. Like the rich man in the Gospel of St. Luke whose soul was demanded even while he dreamed of bigger barns to hold his wealth, Per Hansa dies close to the edge of the same dream, his frozen body facing west when found the following spring.

II

Literary historian Percy Boynton once observed that Rölvaag's novels had come at a good time when the long accumulation of frontier literature seemed to corroborate Turner's frontier thesis. Boynton's point, however, was not that Rölvaag continued the tradition of James Fenimore Cooper, William Gilmore Simms, Timothy Flint, James Hall, Edward Eggleston, Joseph Kirkland and William Allen White—all frontier novelists of sorts. Nor did he interpret Rölvaag as one who depicted the process of Americanization according to Turner's thesis. Instead, what he saw in Rölvaag's work was the Westerner not as a conqueror of the frontier but as one conquered by it.[6] Boynton failed to trace the implications in Turner's statement that the frontier was closed, but he did assert that Rölvaag had significantly shifted away from the American Dream. Closer to Rölvaag's treatment of the Westerner, especially the newly transplanted European, are Willa Cather's *O Pioneers* and *My Ántonia*. But in the case of both Alexandra Bergson and Ántonia Shimerda, the indomitable heroines in these novels, Willa Cather idealized the immigrant. As a Nebraskan transplanted from Virginia, she knew her people mainly through sympathetic observation. When sympathy and observation came into conflict, sympathy triumphed. This meant, according to Boynton, that Willa Cather was unwilling to resign her characters to their fate, and equally unwilling, therefore, to record the frontier's conquest of the pioneers. The same qualification about Cather's work—and that of other frontier writers like Ruth Suckow, Margaret Wilson and Herbert Quick—supported Vernon Louis Parrington's judgment that Rölvaag, far more than these other writers, displayed "the profound insight and imaginative grasp of theme that gives to *Giants in the Earth* so great a sense of tragic reality."[7]

Still another student of the American West, Henry Steele Commager, called *Giants* "the most penetrating and mature depictment of the westward movement in our literature." But Commager adds that this movement has none of the romanticism associated with a proud epic of man's conquest of earth. In Rölvaag's novels, "the westward movement . . . becomes the tragedy of earth's humbling of man." Of all tragedies, Commager writes, "the most poignant is that of futility. . . . And futility is the moral of *Giants in the Earth*."[8]

These readers saw *Giants* as unmistakable tragedy, the same genre that included *Peder Victorious*, published in 1929. What is necessary now is to see the entire trilogy as tragedy, the most sustained in American frontier literature. If a single symbol is depicted in these three novels, it is again that of the closed frontier, the stone wall that obtrudes in the *hilder* vision or a magic ring appearing to Beret early in the first novel. This circle lay on the horizon and extended upward into the sky, or, in slightly different imagery, "it was like a chain inclosing the king's garden, that prevented it from bearing fruit. . . . And those who were strong enough to break through were only being enticed still farther to their destruction!"

To Beret the ring represented the limits of human exploration. To go beyond—as Per Hansa tried to do—was to trespass into awesome precincts of mystery and to invite one's destruction through pride. This ring also symbolized a psychological border beyond which lay the unknown, the wild, the desolate and the dark forces of the mind. To go farther west was to intensify these psychological feelings. As Beret knew, the journey west was like getting lost within one's own inner prairies, a far more precarious adventure than fording rivers and fighting snowstorms. Still another significance associated with the closed frontier in this trilogy was that of cultural entanglements, the kind the second-generation immigrant confronted as he learned that his father's utopian dreams of America as a great and democratic "melting pot" had little connection with the dirty business of politics or the sometimes ugly conflicts between differing ethnic and religious groups.

The ingenious way Rölvaag presented the overall tragedy was to see it in these three aspects: First, Per Hansa, closest to an epic figure in his superhuman strength both in working and in dreaming, dies a tragic figure, unfulfilled in either. His tragedy rests in what he demands of himself in relation to fate, or in relation to the prairies and to their strange and overwhelming might. With his whole heart he summoned the courage to found a kingdom, but the cosmic powers he sought to conquer were his nemesis, freezing him in their icy grasp, then leaving him a putrid corpse in the spring thaw. Second, Beret's tragic drama is played out not on the Dakota prairies but amid those prairies within.[9] Try as she would to curtain the windows from these dreadful vistas or, as protection, to keep close to those few possessions like the trunk she brought from Norway; dream as she would of the old Norwegian churchyard "enclosed by a massive stone wall, broad and heavy"—a wall "more reliable" than anything she could imagine—she, who feared the great stillness of the prairies more than anyone and who longed for some kind of wall to hide behind, was bereft of all security except a severe Lutheranism. Beret's is the tragedy of deracination, cultural uprootedness, separation from language and tradition without any psychological moorings to compensate. Third, the tragedy Peder comes to know is the fraudulence of hope in America as a cultural melting pot where immigrants of diverse backgrounds can start anew to build a harmonious society.

Peder rebels against old Norwegian traditions and turns his back on the God of his fathers. Representing the new American whose traditions are no deeper than the American experience itself, Peder carries out his rebellion by marrying Susie Doheny, an Irish Catholic. "Wait until we get to the end of the world," Peder says to her, "then I'll tell you all manner of beautiful things!" "Are we going to the end of the world?" she replies. "Of course we are!"[10] But as Rölvaag's somber trilogy grinds on, the struggle between man and nature gives way to the business of human relationships between Peder and Susie, representatives of two strongly opposing cultures. This struggle becomes the central focus of the entire trilogy. The question is not whether the immigrant pioneer can subdue nature or fate but whether, freed from the past, he can build a society commensurate with his dreams. Here is the test of vaunted American freedom. Peder hopes to clear the road of worm-eaten barriers, including, he says in *Peder Victorious*, the "high walls" of racial and cultural prejudice. He hopes that through science, progress, independence of thought, even through politics the Promised Land can be reached. Far more than the first-generation immigrant, American-born Peder represents the truly liberated citizen with no heritage save what the frontier instilled. But Peder learns the consequences of striving to recreate man and society, of breathing too deeply the air of independence. Ignoring what Santayana once called "the fatal antiquity of human nature,"[11] Peder learns that the conflicting prejudices embodied in his Norwegian mother and his Irish father-in-law are his and Susie's inheritance too.

The frontier experience that Peder and Susie share does not reconcile their cultural differences. Instead, Peder's insistence that reconciliation take place only according to what he considers his enlightened common sense drives him to smash Susie's precious crucifix and her vessel for holy water, crunching them viciously beneath his heel, and then to destroy her rosary, bead by bead, grinding them in the same way. Susie cowers horrified by what she witnesses, but Peder who is now content sleeps soundly only to find in the morning Susie's departing note: "Now I've lived the Blessed Day, I've been to the end of the World and have found out what it looks like. I'll never go near there again, because it is an accursed place." The trilogy ends, the name—Peder Victorious—a tragic mockery. One wonders what further mockery Rölvaag intended to depict in still a fourth volume, never written, one which would take Peder to the bloodstained battlefields of World War I where an even greater dream vanished.

III

This tension between the epic and the tragic, *hilder* and the closed wall, supplies the dynamics of the trilogy; it also infused Rölvaag's thinking even before he had emigrated to America. Born and reared on the tiny island of Donna, only five miles from the Arctic Circle, Rölvaag was well acquainted with the unfathomable ways of nature, with the incredible beauty of its summer nights as well as the treachery of its winter storms. In one such storm in 1893 several fisherman from Rölvaag's village drowned, and he barely escaped. From this experience grew a resentment against destiny not unlike the frightening inner world depicted the same year by the Norwegian Edvard Munch in his painting "The Scream." The insidious resentment changed to outrage when in the spring of 1920 Rölvaag's five-year-old son, Paul Gunnar, was drowned while at play. Some eleven years later, three months before his own death, he wrote to his friend, G. F. Newburger:

> "It's nothing but a common, ordinary, romantic lie that we are the 'captains of our own souls'! Nothing but one of those damned phrases. Just look back over your own life and see how much you have captained! You have been nothing but an ordinary hand in the fo'castle. And that's what we all are."[12]

This brooding note, this melancholy and repressed bitterness, darkened Rölvaag's thinking even while he dedicated nearly twenty-five years of his life to making his own Norwegian people see that to follow an ideal makes them agents in "the creative power of God." Before finishing his undergraduate education he thought of this ideal in terms of *conservation* and *growth:* that true culture in America meant the old must always be preserved in the new. This ideal remained paramount, and even toward the end of his life he spoke of its preservation as "a people's divine creative mission." Yet there was the haunting question that he asked himself again and again: "Must an idealist always die before his thoughts bear fruit?"[13]

What Rölvaag thought to be an American ideal he also interpreted as a personal one. One lesson he learned from his favorite writer, Henrik Ibsen, was that "only when the individual fulfills himself can a new society be possible." But from Ibsen he learned another lesson as well. This was the lesson found in *Brand* that free exercise of will results in disaster. It is not surprising that at St. Olaf College Rölvaag's two favorite courses came to be Ibsen's dramas and Norwegian immigration. Nor is it any less surprising that as a boy in Nordland he and his brother Johan, along with two village friends, John and Hans Heitman, read aloud together Kierkegaard's *Either-Or*. Rölvaag was no stranger to ambivalence. The great All or Nothing theme in Ibsen and Kierkegaard is the same tension Rölvaag saw in the immigrants' destiny in America.

Before he polarized this ambivalence in the characters of Per Hansa and Beret, Rölvaag gave ample hints of the direction he was taking. His first published novel, *Amerika-Breve* (*Letters from America*, 1912), consists of twenty-three letters written by fictional Per Smevik to his father and brother in Norway and collected by the father's friend, Paal Mörck, whose name serves as the novel's pseudonymous author. The letters, based on those Rölvaag wrote home during his early years in South Dakota, thematically juxtapose the new and the old cultures. Strong and ambitious, Per Smevik, who can be called Rölvaag's first Per Hansa figure, stands opposite the old world figure of Mörck whose name means *dark*. Using the same pseudonym, Rölvaag brought bolder strokes to this conflict of cultures in his next novel, *Paa Glemte Veie* (*On Forgotten Paths*, 1914). This novel dramatizes the clash between Chris Larsen, a hard-fighting pioneer who makes a fortune in farming and land speculation, and his physically and temperamentally delicate wife, Magdalene, who stands as Rölvaag's first Beret figure, one who longs for the past. Sympathetic as Rölvaag was to the hardy conqueror of the prairie, this novel makes clear the writer's equally strong feelings for the sensitive, often helpless immigrant who is psychologically unable to cope with frontier life. As for Chris Larsen, who indeed seems able to cope with it, the fact that he survived when his upturned wagon brought death to Magdalene does not blunt the irony that he is later crippled by his runaway horse team. As an invalid he can only wonder what profit his greed has brought him.

For six years after the publication of *On Forgotten Paths* Rölvaag wrote nothing more significant than textbooks and occasional poems and sketches. But with World War I over, his textbook projects completed, the burgeoning of Norwegian literature with Sigrid Undset, Olaf Duun and Johan Bojer, and with the tragic death of his son, Rölvaag snapped out of his lethargy and once again undertook full-length fiction, this time *To Tullinger* (*Two Fools*, 1920), later revised as *Pure Gold* (1930). Once again his theme was greed, though the deeper issue concerned the consequences of cultural rootlessness, the abandoning of the gentler refinements for material opportunities afforded by the New World. This time it is the male character Louis Houglum who harbors respect for tradition, and it is his wife Lizzie who scorns it. Lizzie infects Louis with her avarice and both these second-generation Norwegian-Americans go the way of debasing greed. New traditions replace the old; the kingdom that the Houglums establish duplicates those Rölvaag saw all around him—Gopher Prairie, Winesburg, Zenith, Spoon River, Tilbury—kingdoms of petty materialism, greed, smugness and lost souls.

On his more creative levels of vision Rölvaag perceived the gaping disparity between American promise and American reality. In his next novel, which immediately precedes the trilogy, he brought to this disparity tightly controlled, artistic handling. "I have put more of myself into that book than into any other," he once said.[14] Called *Laengselens Baat* (*Boat of Longing*, 1921), it was an immigrant's story, set not on the prairie but in a hostile urban world. Rölvaag once spoke of the story as "the American *Book of Lamentations*," signifying to him the whole tragic pattern of immigration.[15]

The central point in this novel is the price Nils Vaag, the young Norwegian who finds his way to Minneapolis, pays for leaving his home in Norway. Not only does he discover that his values conflict with America's materialism but that amid the vulgarity and squalor of the city his "boat of longing" will never be anything but a Great Northern train taking him to yet another city where, on its busiest corner, he can only stand "searching and searching, like a lone gull perched watchful on some bold headland round which the ocean current runs swift."[16] This loneliness is more than that of a lost immigrant in an alien city. It is a cleavage of cultures and of generations. To underscore this fact Nil's father, who comes to America to look for his son, gets no farther than Ellis Island where he is told that because he lacks the necessary papers, he must turn back. Old Jo Persa, the father, is then "led through passageway after passageway, out across an open space, down another passage and in through another door, where a key [is] turned on him." There he will wait for his "boat of longing"—another crowded steamer taking him away from the land of his son.

When Rölvaag wrote the trilogy, his loyalties wavered between the New World and the Old, between what he often called the "surface" and the "hidden" in American life. It was obvious to him that the nation's official voice proclaimed the former. Theodore Roosevelt in *The Strenuous Life*, published in 1900, boasted of great deeds and great men. And who better than the Captains of Industry represented the fulfillment of the pioneering struggle? Some American writers, however, fixed their attention on the other side of life even as had some European observers, notably Tocqueville, who predicted that American literature would concentrate less on surface action than on passions and ideas. Of course the great nineteenth-century explorers of these dark realms were Poe, Hawthorne, Melville, Twain and James, all of whom in one way or another recognized the ambivalence in American life but chose to journey where the official voices were not heard. Rölvaag leaned in the same direction, wishing to probe what lay beneath the American enterprise.

Rölvaag's great themes in the trilogy were ostensibly to be the Westward Movement and Immigration. These were the subjects that had preoccupied him from the day he first left Norway in 1896, and he had been personally involved in them ever since. But in the summer of 1922 at Big Island Lake in the northern Minnesota woods where he had built a small cabin, he settled down to undertake that other theme as well: the human cost of the nation's enterprise. What made this deeper, hidden theme important to Rölvaag was again his own ambivalence toward it. Did American success justify the cost? Considering the cost, could one say the pioneers had been successful at all? Despite the obvious evidence bespeaking their triumph, did not an irrepressible tragedy darken the full story?

Physical hardships were one kind of cost. As Parrington noted, Rölvaag was sensitive to the people broken by the frontier, "the great army of derelicts who failed and were laid away . . . in forgotten graves."[17] *Their Fathers' God* opens with the words "No hope," the stark fact that many settlers who no longer had the resolve to face repeated crop failure chose to return to civilization rather than bury their children on the prairie. The scorching heat and the parched, crusted land that Rölvaag describes in this opening scene, and, moreover, the caravans shambling *eastward*, each wagon carrying little more than broken hopes, give evidence that the Myth of the Garden had another side to it. In *Virgin Land*, Henry Nash Smith called this other side the "desert," literally the western prairies higher and closer to the Rockies and drier. But the "desert" had its symbolic meaning as well—a place of poverty and grinding toil, futile dreams and broken promises. On the deepest level it was where the immigrant pioneer faced the fact that he was a stranger even among his own people.

To Rölvaag this was the greatest cost of empire building, this loss of a fatherland and of the spiritual associations it nurtured. In Rölvaag's words:

We came away from our own country and became strangers to our own people. Our pulse can no longer beat in rhythm with the hearts of our own people. We have become strangers—strangers to the people we forsook and strangers to the people we came to. . . . The people we forsook, we remain apart from, and the people we came to, we also remain apart from. We have thus ceased to be an integral part of a larger whole; we have become something by ourselves, something torn off, without any organic connection either here or there. Herein lies the tragedy of emigration.[18]

This was the tragedy Beret knew best. Continually measuring the achievements of Per Hansa, Peder and her neighbors against the cost, she best understands alienation as the essence of that cost. It is not only that her three children come to speak English rather than Norwegian, nor even that Peder, the first born in Spring Creek, scoffs at her Norwegian ideas. That she finally becomes a stranger to him suggests still only a portion of the loss she feels. What she essentially loses is her Norwegian soul. This is what America finally demands; this is the price Beret has to pay. Torn loose from her kindred and fatherland, Beret has no place to go; by the time of the second novel "she saw no escape." On sleepless nights she fashions a recurring image:

She saw herself sitting on a lone rock far out at sea. The surf sucked and boomed. . . . Little by little the surf began sucking her feet. A skua kept circling about the rock. That bird hacked rapaciously at dead bodies floating on the surface—always the eyes. . . . Oh, no, America would not be satisfied with getting their bodies only!

Rölvaag grasped the essential irony in America's promise of freedom and independence. He saw that real freedom and real independence were terrifying prospects because their fulfillment demanded not amalgamation of the old and the new but complete severance. While promising glorious rebirth, the American frontier demanded that the immigrant break ties with the past and that here, even in a Garden of Eden, he *must* stay. This was the irony that made Rölvaag's theme especially bitter. The main point in Beret's tragedy is not that she was unable to unite the old and the new; it was that America demanded the sacrifice of the one for the other, and then, after Beret makes the sacrifice, left her adrift in an alien wilderness.

The American promise is one and the same with its terrible cost. This was Rölvaag's answer to the myth of rebirth and to those other hopes engendered in the American West. Independence meant rootlessness from which would come spiritual disintegration regardless of the material prosperity such liberation brings. Disintegration is Beret's breakdown. What Rölvaag leaves us with is an immigrant who has paid the full price. More tragic than Per Hansa, who gives his body to the prairies, Beret gives her Norwegian soul in exchange for nothing more than the prospect that Peder, in his rebellion against the sustaining heritage she has sacrificed, will stand strangely alienated from the past, just as she stands apart from the present. Bereft of supporting links, Beret was unable to remake her soul, a transformation Rölvaag said was demanded of every immigrant in the New World. Rebirth, he added, "forever will be beyond the power of the average man," who may give up the old, at the price of spiritual death, but who cannot master the new. Adamant on this point, Rölvaag insisted that the immigrant, "especially the Nordic," cannot uproot himself and move to a new land without paying the ultimate price, the sacrifice of his cultural soul.[19]

It was Rölvaag's passionate idea that a people can grow only if they are one with their soil and their historical roots. These "hidden" qualities, he thought, supply the spiritual energy by which a transplanted people sustain their collective aspirations in America. It is for this reason that Beret pleads with her children to speak their native language, to attend their Norwegian Lutheran church, and someday to inspire in their own children the same cultural loyalties she was fighting to retain. She knew that schism spelled both cultural and psychological disaster. She knew that people who "turned their backs on their fathers' God were an abomination in the eyes of the

Lord." This was her parting admonishment as she lay dying, with both Peder and Susie uncomprehendingly looking on. Her sense of dependency—cultural as well as religious—was what the open frontier spirit demanded she relinquish. That she depended upon her Norwegian roots as well as faith in a sovereign God left her a stranger in a land where frontierism repudiated these human dependencies. The trilogy's final chapter ("Father, Forgive Them—!") leaves little doubt as to how Rölvaag resolved the *hilder* vision that sent this immigrant family to seek a new world.

Even though Rölvaag's sympathies are plainly with Beret and her desolate psychological landscape, it is with Peder that he must finally reckon. Per Hansa's indomitable will and Beret's brooding sense of futility converge in Peder, born on Christmas Day, 1873. For Per Hansa the son Peder symbolizes victory, for Beret he is "symbol of sin." This dichotomy recalls the contrast between Per Hansa's swelling optimism, his epic strength and pride, and Beret's guilt. The dichotomy also serves to place Peder firmly between other forces as well. He stands between Per Hansa's quest for the All and Beret's vision of Nothingness. Peder turns away from his mother's preoccupation with the past, but his own visionary future, patterned after his father's dreams, carries him no further than the unbending circumstances of the present. Standing between Norwegian Lutheranism and Irish Catholicism, hoping that their convergence will strengthen his own Americanism, he yet must live with the fact that *his* own son, called Petie, was first clandestinely baptized Peder Emmanuel by Beret and Sörine, then later Patrick St. Olaf in the Catholic church at Susie's instigation. Other dichotomies clash in Peder, most tellingly in *Their Fathers' God*. Born of the soil and growing to manhood as one who shared the farmers' discontent with eastern financiers, Peder nevertheless repudiated the Populists' struggle, and in his campaign for district commissioner in South Dakota he found himself on the side of Republicanism represented by William McKinley and Marcus Hanna. As if this incongruity were not enough, Peder also confronted the shattering accusations of Tom McDougal, his political opponent. In the crowded schoolroom where neighbors for miles around had come to hear the pre-election oratory, McDougal mockingly reminded the audience that Peder's dead mother had spent her last months as a "lunatic," that Peder himself was a freethinker who "didn't give two whoops for either God or the devil," and that Peder's wife had had to sneak his son away for secret baptism. Standing helplessly amid these vilifications, which set the new tone of American politics, Peder wanted nothing more than "to vomit." No longer were the issues clear-cut and the political tactics honorable. To Peder it seemed that America now contradicted the ideals upon which it had been built. Like a sudden blast, McDougal's words sent these ideals "whirling around and around." And as if for the first time Peder saw things and heard things he previously would have thought impossible.

It is after this public nightmare that Peder returns home to Susie and in blind rage smashes her crucifix and rosary. Freed at last from these traditional symbols of human dependency Peder stands alone with neither wife nor son, with neither religious nor cultural roots. His victory is no less a mockery than his freedom. In the character of Peder Victorious, Rölvaag gave his narrative of immigration and America's Westward Movement its final tragic significance. Like a Greek chorus, Nikoline speaks to Peder of America: "Beautiful...and terrible, too." To Peder's question, "terrible in Paradise?" she answers: "There was one standing there, one with a flaming sword. . . . I wasn't allowed to get in!" It is this lesson that Peder learns.

8

California, Nathanael West and the Journey's End

AS IF by destiny, Walt Whitman's song calling for all Americans to enlarge their souls harmonized perfectly with President James K. Polk's intention to enlarge America's soil. By the time the poet's song was heard, America indeed had swelled to the Pacific. The achievement following Polk's inauguration was remarkable: Texas in 1845, the Oregon Territory and California in 1848. As counterpoint were the pulse-tingling words "manifest destiny," handily introduced in 1845 by the editor of the *New York Morning News*, John L. O'Sullivan, who wrote of "our manifest destiny to overspread and to possess the whole continent which Providence has given us." By the end of the century this moral mandate sent Americans seeking still other continents which, perhaps, Providence had also given them. But within this continent alone, the mandate was sufficient reason to allow the United States to fulfill its role as mother of freedom, a role that in the West meant liberating those people suffering under the bondage of England and Mexico. As one western crusader wrote of the Mexican Californians: "They are only a grade above the aborigines, and like them will be compelled by the very nature of things, to yield to the swelling tide of Anglo-Saxon adventure." The story is, of course, rich in drama. In looking back over the days of the Oregon and California trails, the Gold Rush, the railroads, and all those dreamers of the frontier dream, one must agree with critic Edmund Wilson, who said that California, especially since we took it away from the Mexicans, "had always presented itself to Americans as one of the strangest and most exotic of our adventures."[1]

It would be in California, if at all, where the American frontier dream would be authenticated. Here was the literal end of the trail, and here the Great Promise had to be revealed. Suggestive of this fulfillment is Bayard Taylor's account of the Santa Clara Valley. Commissioned by Horace Greeley to report on the California Gold Rush to the *New-York Tribune*, Taylor wrote that "the unvarying yellow hue of mountain and plain, except where they were transversed by broad belts of dark-green timber, gave a remarkable effect to the view." The mountains "seemed to have arrayed themselves in cloth of gold, as if giving testimony to the royal metal [in] which their veins abound." The more prosaic reasons pioneers headed west, and on to California, are well known. Ray Allen Billington uses the term, "abundancy motivation," meaning "a desire to find new pleasures, gratifications, experiences, and achievements." Most of these reasons had to do in some way with economic or social advantage, explained by Frederick Jackson Turner's "safety valve" theory and the mobility enjoyed by those who went west. But there was that other motivation as well, the one that spelled the call of the wild, the unknown, the mystical. California's gold served as the perfect symbol. For his millions of readers Zane Grey's explanation was as good as any: that men in his western land could come "to a supreme proof of the evolution of man, to a realization of God."[2]

To find in California what is strange and exotic is also to discover its tragic groundwork. With desperate effort the frontiersman had crossed the continent; and, decades later, with similar effort, the man from Iowa had saved his money or had planned his career so that, at last, he could go to California to live the good life. As if the continent tilted toward Southern California, the people journeyed to Los Angeles, which, like some vast organism, spread out for miles while its population increased from some fifty thousand in 1890 to over half a million thirty years later. The prospering oil, film and aircraft industries were in Los Angeles, but people came also to wrest nothing less than human fulfillment and God's special providence for America. By the 1920s, as one historian says, California had come to be

> a sort of middle-class Methodist paradise, with enough sunshine and oranges to give color, enough innovations in the way of airplanes and automobiles and cafeterias to lend excitement, and enough ruggedness—with its jack rabbits and stingarees [stingrays] and hiking trails and surf bathing—to provide adventure.

For the non-Methodists, life in Los Angeles promised to be "one long cocktail of orange blossoms, ocean beaches, and Spring Street." Intent upon creating an exotic Mediterranean culture, enthusiasts named their towns Arcadia, Hesperia, Morocco, Verona; Abbot Kinney spent a fortune developing "Venice," a cultural center near Pasadena complete with canals, weeping willow trees, gondolas, singing gondoliers and imported Venetian pigeons; and with the help of Henry Huntington and others, Frank Miller of Riverside built Mission Inn, called "the Alhambra" of the Pacific Coast by its many renowned visitors who sat quietly in the shade of lemon trees and bougainvillea to listen to mission bells.[3]

All these efforts to create a paradise where dreams come true, where physical and spiritual health is restored after one's long years on the severe Nebraska or Dakota prairie, and where fullness of life has something to do with exotic surroundings kept pace with the flow of newcomers. Los Angeles became the mecca for cultists of all description—"sick survivors of New England transcendentalism," said Paul Jordan-Smith, a long-time Los Angeles spokesman who, in his essay, "Los Angeles: Ballyhooers in Heaven," noted that the milder climate enabled them "to keep the illusion that they have conquered disease through spiritual power." During the 1920s the "religious awakening" in Los Angeles reached such proportions that legislation finally forced soothsayers, fortune-tellers and swamis to operate under license. As the oasis for divine healing, occult science, reincarnation and astrological revelations, the city in 1926 had seven separate churches of the American Theosophical Society and twenty-one churches of the National Spiritualist Association. Living in palaces of opulent optimism or surging along Spring Street, the people seized at whatever offered uplift, be it the faith of some newly arrived prophet, or only a pamphlet announcing still another real estate subdivision, this one perhaps named Eve's Garden. As Paul Jordan-Smith observed, Los Angeles was "less a city of angels than a paradise of realtors and a refuge for the rheumatics." The point, as he notes, is that the newcomers hoped to find their Promised Land in Los Angeles, their "American Port Said," and instead discovered a population of "Iowa farmers and sunburned old maids in an endless chain of cafeterias, movie palaces and state picnics." The city of angels was "just as dull as the traditional kingdom of heaven."[4]

Wherein lies the tragedy? Simply and profoundly in the disparity between illusion and reality, between the promise and its denial. In the American Westward Movement, California came to symbolize the logical conclusion of America itself. Not only had a continent been crossed but in the West lived a new breed (some even called them a new species, endowed, said occultists P. D. Ouspensky, Annie Besant and others, with "higher consciousness") that had sloughed off the past with its stale traditions and built a civilization more uniquely American than anything in the Ohio Valley or the Virginia Piedmont. But if at the trail's end there was only fool's gold, if fulfillment failed to square with expectation, if with unabated frenzy Californians were *still* seeking their Promised Land, then what follows must be despair, first mute, then violent, according to the extent of hope originally proffered. It is this scene of the American Westerner with nowhere left to go, with the frontier closed, with only California at his feet, with shore and waves but no "passage to India," that the pioneer never dared to imagine. The one dream he dared not dream was exactly the one he did not need to dream, for he now confronted the reality that his transcendental self, which had previously been supported by the metaphor of the open frontier, no longer found a safety valve through which to escape. Space had closed in upon him.

It was not merely the need to readjust to a closed-space existence in the literal sense. Living in cities rather than on prairies, accepting more governmental restriction, getting along within complex communication and transportation systems, coping with automation, or adjusting to a thousand other situations unique to twentieth-century urban America have little to do with what it means to face the closed frontier as a metaphor of tragedy. Nor was it that Westerners had not asked the fateful questions about existence. It was instead that they had not asked such questions in terms of their own existence. It became obvious, after finding California something less than what the rainbow had promised, that Westerners still would not force questions upon existence but would rather manufacture the dreamworld they so desperately sought, or else destroy the dream factories, and themselves in a single apocalyptic holocaust.

II

If it is legitimate to trace the Westward Movement to its logical end in California, and if the whole incremental symbolism of this movement can be given a California setting, then the work of Nathanael West must be read as a profound interpretation of how the great myth of the West comes to an end. Many writers of stature have written about California. One immediately thinks of F. Scott Fitzgerald and John Steinbeck, or such satirists as Aldous Huxley and Evelyn Waugh. One also thinks of all those writers who spent their last years in Southern California: Julian Hawthorne in Pasadena; Hamlin Garland and Theodore Dreiser who found Hollywood culture perfect for their spiritualistic pursuits; a potpourri of other writers including Upton Sinclair, Edgar Rice Burroughs, Gene Stratton Porter, Rupert Hughes and Zane Grey; and a handful of foreign authors including Huxley, Franz Werfel and, for a time, Thomas Mann. Yet, strangely enough, Nathanael West was like none of these, just as his *The Day of the Locust* (1939) brings the frontier to a close as does no other American novel.

The critical attention West has received since his death in California in 1940 makes clear that his works—especially *Miss Lonelyhearts* (1933) and *The Day of the Locust*—have found an important place in American literature, primarily because they capture the inevitable tragedy in American frontierism. West's writing is not restricted to this American theme, nor does it place him among only American writers of his own day. Several scholars suggest strong resemblances between West and Dostoevsky; or they see West as living in the haunted castles of Salvador Dali and Giorgio de Chirico; they find echoes of T. S. Eliot's *The Waste Land* nearly everywhere in West. Even West himself in his writing of *Miss Lonelyhearts* acknowledges indebtedness to William James, John Bunyan and Leo Tolstoy. In fact, Nathanael West has contributed greatly to an American view of tragedy. And, as this view relates to the dominant metaphor of the closed frontier, his position in American literature grows ever stronger.

Even in his independence, his work reflects interesting similarities to that of Sherwood Anderson and F. Scott Fitzgerald. Randall Reid, for example, gives considerable attention to the way *The Day of the Locust* and *Winesburg, Ohio* are similar. Like Homer Simpson in West's novel, Anderson's characters long to return to Eden, which "beckons somewhere in the distance." But at the moment of release—defined as "expressive communion with someone else"—they are irrevocably thwarted, and the tragic fact is that in both Anderson and West, "the grotesque is normal." As for West and Fitzgerald, one discovers many similarities as well as the uncanny coincidence that the two writers died only a few miles apart on successive days. Both men came from American minorities, one Jewish and the other Irish Catholic; both went to Paris after college; both created unforgettable images of the waste land, one of old movie lots and the other of the Valley of Ashes; both wrote "last" novels about Hollywood; both, observes David D. Galloway, had "an agonized sense of the ironies of life, and their heroes all embarked on the fatal race for a green light or a silver screen image that continually receded before them," and, according to Edmund Wilson, who epitomized eastern critical opinion, both failed "to get the best out of their best years" because, in part at least, they succumbed to Hollywood "with its already appalling record of talent depraved and wasted."[5]

Instead of succumbing to Hollywood, however, West found there the instant symbol for the theme he had been developing ever since his first novel, *The Dream Life of Balso Snell* (1931). The same relationship with Hollywood prevails in his style, which takes on the kind of radical distortion he later found pervading life in Southern California. More than either Anderson or Fitzgerald, West artistically wove something monstrous and misshapen into his novels, the same qualities the French surrealist painters brought to their work. Like them West recreated a twisted, demented world. It is true he did this before he saw Hollywood, for even in his first two books, *Balso Snell* and *Miss Lonelyhearts*, this kind of bizarre world exists. But his trip to Hollywood in 1933 and his return for good in 1935 confirmed the American correlative. His third novel, *A Cool Million* (1934), demolishes the American Horatio Alger myth, and *The Day of the Locust* does the same to the frontier myth. West's last novel incorporates many of the concepts, themes and styles of his earlier work, but the author uses Hollywood as the locus for this, his darkest and most tragic scene. In Hollywood, West transmogrifies his apocalyptic theme into something uniquely American. One might speculate how far he would have carried his dark ideas, but West was killed in an automobile accident on December 22, 1940, when he was only thirty-seven years old.

III

Balso Snell was published the same year (1931) Nathanael West legally changed his name from Nathan Weinstein, although he had written the novel six years earlier when he was living in Paris. Considering that he was only twenty-two at the time, it is remarkable that this first novel should have contained the key to all his later works. It is equally striking that he chose the name he did for himself. When questioned about this, West answered, "Horace Greeley said, 'Go West young man.' So I did."[6] Since West was always careful in choosing names for his fictional characters, he could not have missed what his new name implied. As an explicit metaphor in his last novel, it also announces the theme found in all four novels and introduced by Balso Snell with the opening epigram: "After all, my dear fellow, life, Anaxagoras has said, is a journey." What preoccupied West in this key novel was the nature of the journey.[7]

The one Balso takes seems little more than an outrageous parody. After entering the "mystic portal," ("O Anus Mirabilis!") of the Greeks' famous wooden horse, Balso sees "a beautiful Doric prostate gland"; he enters "the large intestine" and, while talking with his guide about art as "sublime excrement," makes headway "up the tube." Down "the great tunnel" he comes upon Maloney the Areopagite who, "naked except for a derby in which thorns were sticking," was trying "to crucify himself with thumbtacks." After listening to Maloney's biography of Saint Puce, a flea who lived in the armpit of Christ, Balso turns "a bend in the intestine" and encounters a boy with a diary supposedly written for his teacher, Miss McGeeney. The entries are mostly his "Crime Journal," one signed "John Raskolnikov Gilson" and another containing the boy's long Dostoevskian dreamlike account of how he murdered an idiot neighbor. Putting the diary aside, Balso takes up a pamphlet, again supposedly written by Miss McGeeney's young student, who reflects upon the death of Saniette, a smart and sophisticated woman representing the type of audience for whom he, the youthful student, writer and actor, sees himself as "a tragic clown," one who must "burlesque the mystery of feeling at its source" and then "laugh at the laugh." Balso next spies Miss McGeeney herself—"a middle aged woman dressed in a mannish suit and wearing hornrimmed glasses"—who succeeds in grabbing Balso and forcing him to listen to her new biography, *Samuel Perkins: Smeller*. He finally frees himself, hits her "a terrific blow in the gut," throws her into a fountain, and then wonders if the only people inhabiting the wooden horse are "writers in search of an audience."

He next encounters Janey Davenport, called "the Lepi," a hunchback with a "beautiful, hydrocephalic forehead," who agrees to "yield" to Balso after he kills her lover, Beagle Darwin. Nothing comes from this arrangement except that Balso reads two letters Beagle had written to Janey explaining that he, Beagle, refused to take her to Paris because he was convinced the trip would result in her suicide. Actually the letters recapitulate her hypothetical suicide and Beagle's feigned madness following it. At this point in his journey Balso "awoke" to see Miss McGeeney, who explains that she has written the two letters as part of a novel. She identifies herself as Mary, Balso's old friend. They make love, his ejaculation being nothing more than a wet dream as the novel ends.

Fantastic parody that this novel is, West is deadly serious about the subjects he treats. There is no mistaking his indictment against art and the patronizing art-lovers over whose heads, he says at one point, the ceiling of the theater ought to be made to open and "cover the occupants with tons of loose excrement." His position against church and culture, especially the commercialization of both, is equally petulant. West subjects "Home and Duty, Love and Art" to scathing parody, sustained throughout by what Balso Snell's initials clearly stand for.

On a deeper level West condemns whatever gets in the way of honest feeling. Here is his castigation of literature, if what one knows about "Death, Love, Beauty" or "Love, Life, Death" consists merely of words that protect one from experience. Equally intolerable as protection against reality is philosophic idealism, which reconciles the Plural into the Singular, does away with beginnings and ends, and appropriates the circle as its illusory symbol of human existence. Such monism, Balso reads in the pamphlet, is like Saniette's "hiding under the blankets of her hospital bed and invoking the aid of Mother [Mary Baker] Eddy . . . 'I won't die! I'm getting better and better. I won't die.'" In the same way Beagle Darwin speculates about ways to avoid the fact of death as he imagines Janey Davenport's suicide. His alternatives are to remain "cold, calm, collected, almost stolid"; to stay in his ivory tower of thought and refuse to disturb "that brooding white bird, my spirit"; to call himself the "Buffoon of the New Eternities" and, like Mary Baker Eddy, preach that life is merely "the absence of Death" and Death merely "the absence of Life"; or to feign either sadness or madness. In short, like a tragic clown, to "convert everything into fantastic entertainment," finally laughing at the laugh itself.

At the heart of the novel is Dante's dark wood, described in the pamphlet and the two letters Balso reads. Here is where Balso's journey takes him. "It seems to me," he reads in the pamphlet,

> as though all the materials of life—wood, glass, wool, skin—are rubbing against my sty, my cold sore and my pimples; rubbing in such a way as not to satisfy the itch or convert irritation into active pain, but so as to increase the size of the irritation, magnify it and make it seem to cover everything—hysteria, despair.

For this condition, for this irritation of the spirit, there is neither relief nor escape: no Keats, music, mathematics or architecture. This tragic condition is not to be surmounted or transcended. No mystic revelation, no pantheistic apotheosis will come either to justify or to annul it. Only by playing the clown can one cope with it. And, asks Beagle Darwin, "What is more tragic than the role of clown?" The clown pretends the illusions are real, but he knows that

> Life is but the span from womb to tomb; a sigh, a smile; a chill, a fever; a throe of pain, a spasm of volupty [*sic*]: then a gasping for breath and the comedy is over, the song is ended, ring down the curtain, the clown is dead.

The novel depicts human birth, signaled not by the Three Kings, the Dove, or the Star of Bethlehem, but only by "old Doctor Haasenschweitz who wore rubber gloves and carried a towel over his arm like a waiter." "The tragedy of all of us" is that we are only human, that our father came not as the mythical swan, bull or shower of gold; he came only from the bathroom and "with his pants unsupported by braces." We were conceived, not like Christ, Dionysus or Gargantua, but like the deformed Janey Davenport—"in an offhand manner on a rainy afternoon."

The crucial ambiguity of the novel is whether or not Balso understands what he has read in the pamphlet and in Beagle Darwin's two letters. Does he know where his journey has taken him, and does he discover what it means to play the role of tragic clown? It seems clear that Balso's mystical experience at the end of the novel when the "Two became One," paralleling the moment when he and Mary McGeeney copulate, can only be West's parodical *coup de grâce* suggesting something more closely akin to Sartre's horrible ecstasy. If, then, Balso Snell's dreamworld is one of total delusion, if what he takes as a miracle is only hysteria and despair, then the ambiguity perfectly serves the novel's irony: Balso Snell journeys to what for him is meaningless. His journey to the tragic depths brings him nothing more than the grandest of all illusions—his "shout of triumph . . . victorious, relieved."

More than Balso, Miss Lonelyhearts, in West's next novel, understands that life is a "stinking business." To those who endure it because they are either too witless or, like Melville's Bartleby, too honest to run from it, Miss Lonelyhearts compassionately murmurs, "Ah, humanity." But in his public statements, printed as advice in his newspaper lovelorn column, Miss Lonelyhearts offers much more. To Sick-of-it-all and Desperate and Brokenhearted and Disillusioned-with-tubercular-husband he writes that "Life *is* worth while, for it is full of dreams and peace, gentleness and ecstasy, and faith that burns like a clear white flame on a grim dark altar." At the same time he knows his words fail to meet the needs of those persons who seek his help. The words also fail to assuage his own life of quiet desperation. Miss Lonelyhearts' journey is a *via dolorosa*, a forbidding effort to support promises with facts. "Christ is love" is the promise; the letters heaped on his desk each day are the facts. An abyss lies between.

III

If only Miss Lonelyhearts himself could believe the promise, then everything would be simple and the letters extremely easy to answer. But he is caught in the condition of one to whom knowledge and belief are vastly disparate. Various escapes beguile him from this trap: nature, the South Seas, hedonism, art, sex, humanism, marriage and home, even drugs and suicide. Each offers some reconciliation; each answers some of his questions. Instead of peace, however, they leave him with only a strange exhaustion, yet with a desperate compulsion to continue seeking, even though no signs of spring, no "target" in the sky, offer hope.

What makes Miss Lonelyhearts a tragic figure is that in a belittered world he seeks order, Christian order founded on Christ's love. "If you love everything," Miss Lonelyhearts reads in *The Brothers Karamazov*, "you will perceive the divine mystery in things. . . . And you will come at last to love the whole world with an all-embracing love." These words spoken by Father Zossima to Alyosha were now taken by Miss Lonelyhearts into the Dismal Swamp, where he has a vision of the world as a great pawnshop and of himself as one who was appointed to set its litter aright. All the fur coats, diamond rings, watches, shotguns, fishing tackle, mandolins—all this "paraphernalia of suffering"—Miss Lonelyhearts confronts, first arranging everything into a giant phallus, then a diamond, and after these a circle, triangle, square, swastika. Not until he has fashioned a gigantic cross is his vision complete. Each shape symbolizes a *Weltanschauung*. The cross symbolizes his own. His decision to act upon this Christ-dream, to reconcile his actions with the Christ-promise, is the desperate wager. "He had played with this thing ['this Christ business'], but had never allowed it to come alive." His gamble is to battle the world's chaos with love.

This gamble is like the turning point of Melville's novel *Pierre*, when Pierre throws himself upon the Chronometrical instead of the Horological. To Pierre chronometrical standards come to represent "ideas celestial" whereas the horological ones represent "things terrestrial." The analogy is to a

Greenwich chronometer; when it indicates twelve o'clock high noon locally, watches elsewhere will indicate a different time, say, twelve o'clock midnight. Melville says the former "will always" contradict the latter. Thus heavenly wisdom, analogous with chronometrical or absolute time, is earthly folly. Melville explains that, for the human masses, heavenly or chronometrical righteousness "is not only impossible, but would be entirely out of place, and positively wrong" in our horological, everyday and relative world. Christ's injunction, for example, that when struck on one cheek we turn the other is chronometrical; so also his injunction that we give all we have to the poor. The chronometrical and horological conceit teaches that "in things terrestrial [horological] a man must not be governed by things celestial [chronometrical]."[8] If he is, Christ's crucifixion makes clear the consequence.

In *Miss Lonelyhearts* the character Shrike embodies the horological. With terrifying insight he knows the folly of Miss Lonelyhearts' living in this world by the standards of the other. But like Pierre, Miss Lonelyhearts crosses the Rubicon and gambles on the chronometrical. He admits to a "Christ complex," and even though his friends mockingly call him a "leper licker," he declares himself a "humanity lover." In the novel's final chapter, "Miss Lonelyhearts Has a Religious Experience," a mystic vision comes to him as he stares at a figure of Christ hung on his bedroom wall. He sees that the real Christ is "life and light." For a moment his room is "full of grace," his identification with God "complete." He has seen Christian order; his pawnshop world fits together into a beautiful Oneness and he with it.

But like the fateful knocking on the gate in *Macbeth*, a doorbell shatters the vision of Miss Lonelyhearts, who goes to the top of the stairs to watch Peter Doyle, a cripple, trudging up toward him. Fresh from his religious experience, Miss Lonelyhearts takes Doyle for another Desperate, Broken-hearted, Sick-of-it-all, and rushes to embrace him with love. A bullet from the gun of Doyle, who has had his own grievances against Miss Lonelyhearts, sends the deluded savior tumbling down the stairs, down into the very horological world he had thought he could transform. Christian love has been shattered by murderous life.

At the end of their respective journeys both Balso Snell and Miss Lonelyhearts supposedly experience a mystical Oneness with all things. As if absorbed in God and made God, Balso merges with "the One that is all things and yet no one of them" and Miss Lonelyhearts experiences "two rhythms that were slowly becoming one. . . . His heart was the one heart, the heart of God." But nothing in West could be more ironic. Balso's expanded consciousness was only sexual fantasy and Miss Lonelyhearts' Truth is only the stage setting for the real truth, namely, that life is violent, not loving.

One might strenuously argue that Miss Lonelyhearts is a religious saint: he first withdraws from the world in order to correct it, he subdues selfhood, he undergoes a dark night of the soul, and then he finally knows the joy of mystical union with God. To support this interpretation, critic Thomas M. Lorch cites West's statement, found in a short piece West called "Some Notes on Miss L.," that "Miss Lonelyhearts became the portrait of a priest of our time who has a religious experience."[9] It must be noted, however, that in the novel Shrike makes an almost identical observation: "Did I myself not say that the Miss Lonelyhearts are the priests of twentieth-century America?" That Shrike jokes at the hollowness of such priesthood is not too different from the way Nathanael West mockingly brings each of his protagonists' journeys to a dead end. To Miss Lonelyhearts and Lemuel Pitkin in *A Cool Million*, West ironically bestows martyrdom. ("He [Miss Lonelyhearts] smiled at Shrike as the saints are supposed to have smiled at those about to martyr them.") Rather than showing Miss Lonelyhearts as a religious saint, West shows the grotesqueness of this identity. Thinking himself another Christ, Miss Lonelyhearts rushes to make the cripple, Peter Doyle, "whole again," but instead, the savior, felled by the bullet, drags the cripple down with him in a crazy reversal of the resurrection. His mystical union with God and his vision of himself as a savior parallel those of Lemuel Pitkin, another crippled martyr, whose last words before an assassin's bullet found *its* mark were: "I am a clown . . . but there are times when even clowns must grow serious. This is such a time. I. . . ."

IV

In his third novel, *A Cool Million*, written after his 1933 visit to Hollywood, West sends his deluded protagonist, Lemuel Pitkin, on a journey that literally costs him his teeth, an eye, a thumb, his scalp, a leg and finally his life. Comic as this business is, the underlying seriousness concerns West's devastating treatment of American capitalism and his complete renunciation of the myth of the open frontier. Out to seek his fortune like a western Horatio Alger, Lemuel encounters frauds and con men of every description, each carrying out the great American prerogative of free enterprise. Deluded by the notion that others are as innocently engaged as himself, Lemuel goes his way, incredulously finding himself in one dead-end after another. The biggest fraud of all is Nathan "Shagpoke" Whipple, former president of the United States as well as of the Rat River National Bank. It is with "Shagpoke" that the guileless Lemuel goes to California to dig gold, an outrageous adventure that leaves Lemuel without his scalp and a leg; and it is also with him that Lemuel travels "many weary months" as the chief attraction of their tent show, in which Lemuel, showing off his scalped skull, is hailed as the only survivor of the Yuba River massacre. For a while the two adventurers— one as naive as the other is cunning—work for S. Snodgrasse's road show, which features the "Chamber of American Horrors/ Animate and Inanimate/Hideosities." With a gigantic, electrically lighted hemorrhoid in the center, the "inanimate" exhibit displays objects "whose distinction lay in the great skill with which their materials had been disguised": paper made to look like wood, "wood like rubber, rubber like steel, steel like cheese, cheese like glass, and, finally, glass like paper . . . pencil sharpeners that could also be used as earpicks, can openers as hair brushes . . . flower pots that were really victrolas, revolvers that held candy, candy that held collar buttons and so forth." The "animate" part of the show is a pageant showing Quakers "being branded, Indians brutalized and cheated, Negroes sold, children sweated to death." Culminating the pageant is a playlet set first in "a typical American home" where a white-haired grandmother is hoodwinked out of her money by a "sleek salesman," and then on a busy street where the grandmother and her three starved grandchildren lie dead while two laughing millionaires, almost tripping over the corpses, curse "the street cleaning department for its negligence."

Duped, defrauded and literally decimated, Lemuel is still not shaken by what has clearly become an American nightmare, complete with West's surrealism. Lemuel, whose grotesque disfigurement contrasts with his innocence, continues to believe in the American Dream, which West shows as defrauding all Americans who, holding desperately to it, go to California to have it come true. Calling on the "Golden Gates Employment Bureau," Lemuel gratefully takes a job as stooge in still another road show, this one featuring a team of men who in the last act bring out an enormous wooden mallet called "The Works" and proceed to "demolish" him. First his toupee flies off, then his glass eye and false teeth pop out, and finally his wooden leg is knocked into the audience which, at this point, is "convulsed with joy."

In this novel West is working toward the kind of mob violence marking certain scenes in *Huckleberry Finn*. But with West this violence more sharply reflects people ready for catastrophe. These are the people self-justified by their own innocent righteousness. The more fanatically they defend the illusion, the more violently and joyfully they make victims of those who, by their existence alone, vex it. This fanaticism coupled with a suspicion that they themselves are victims of some gigantic fraud brings on the riot marking the end of what Nathanael West saw for the American frontier journey. The sweeping, engulfing violence in West's last novel is only incipient in *A Cool Million*. But its terror is nonetheless real, as seen not only in Lemuel's disfigurement but in the riot "Shagpoke" incited in the name of his fascist National Revolutionary Party, a riot in which southern white Protestant citizens of Beulah raise the Confederate flag on their courthouse staff and then proceed to parade the heads of Blacks on poles, nail a Jew to the door of his hotel room and rape the local Catholic priest's housekeeper.

Unlike Huck Finn, Lemuel has nowhere "to light out" to. Illusory as Huck's escape was, Lemuel's open frontier is an even greater illusion. For Lemuel the frontier was closed even before he started his journey, and his innocence could never survive, let alone be reborn. In Huck's world there was still nature, and there was love between him and Jim. In Lemuel's world neither exists. There is only the chaos of violence, brutality, fanaticism and dissemblance—a closed world in which nature is synthetic and people are hell. The great difference between Huck and Lemuel is that whereas Huck recognized evil for what it was, Lemuel perceives nothing beyond his dreamworld. Huck's innocence felt the crush of reality. Lemuel's innocence, on the other hand, feels nothing, even though he is literally torn apart by the real world. Actually Lemuel's is not innocence at all but a parody of it. Nothing tragic marks Lemuel as a character because he realizes nothing about either himself or his world. Thoroughly duped and deceived he dies a martyr for a cause he neither understands nor upholds. He dies a spokesman for the same forces of destruction that hail him as a martyr, the same forces that are intent upon making America "again American," the kind of fascism that will *have* its American Dream, come fire or brimstone.

That Lemuel Pitkin is not a tragic figure does not mean that West suspended this view in *A Cool Million*. Even though West never created a character of fully tragic dimensions, he did portray what can be called a tragic society. It is also true that he depicted certain characters whose dreams led to tragic consequences. Especially with Miss Lonelyhearts, these consequences are psychologically and spiritually credible. But West's creative insights focus more sharply upon masses than upon individuals. His concern is what happens to a society whose collective dream contradicts reality, and whose only way of confronting a closed frontier is by dreaming it is still open. This is why his insights are peculiarly American. As early as his first novel and his reference in it to Mary Baker Eddy, West identified the society as American, and in his next novel he refers to Miss Lonelyhearts as representative of "the priests of twentieth-century America." The society is unmistakably American in *A Cool Million*, and by the time he wrote *The Day of the Locust*, West concentrates all his vitriol upon a single place, Hollywood, and upon a single dream, the frontier. West's cynicism, anger, mockery and disgust cover the general malaise of the modern era; but it is to the twentieth-century American that he brings his full creative attention. Even though his first three books have their own artistic integrity, they serve as a long prelude to his final masterpiece. All that is in the earlier novels is to be found in *The Day of the Locust* (1939) and the powerful concentration is almost overwhelming. No angrier book in American literature has been written since *The Confidence-Man* and *The Mysterious Stranger*.

V

An inevitability distinguishes West's last novel, as if by fate it was indeed to be his final work. In it the assumptions of the earlier works are not only elaborated but they carry eschatological importance. The masses in *The Day of the Locust* are waiting for the end. They dream with latent "messianic rage" of the last big miracle. No longer are they individually tragic clowns like the characters Abe Kusich and Harry Greener or even little Adore. They are now the "locust" with "wild, disordered minds" and the "awful, anarchic power" to destroy civilization. They are the cultists and mad dreamers, standing before their New Thought shrines and awaiting the apotheosis that the Golden West promised. The sex dream, the Christ dream, the million-dollar dream—all tried and untrue—must now make way for the paradise dream: "Why," says Maybelle Loomis (an old-time Westerner of six years), California is "a paradise on earth."

Like Harry Greener who once restricted his clowning to the stage but who now clowns continuously as "his sole method of defense," the hordes dare not see Hollywood for the dream dump it is. To do so would be, as Lemuel Pitkin discovered, to "grow serious," and at such a moment reality crashes in. In West's novel, society has become clownlike—the fat lady in the yachting cap who goes shopping, not boating, for example; or the man in the Tyrolean hat who returns home from an insurance office, not a mountain. Hollywood, once a stage, is now a way of life, a paradise for masqueraders.

West seems to have had no choice in making Hollywood the setting for this novel. Daniel Aaron points out that West does not merely give a "superficial arraignment of the film colony," nor does he intend "a romantic evocation of Hollywood as epic," after the manner of Evelyn Waugh or F. Scott Fitzgerald. Instead, says Aaron, Hollywood is a "symbol of despair and unfulfillment."[10] It symbolizes the fateful destiny of a society living on illusions.

There is also a terrible inevitability in what Tod Hackett will paint. Hired to learn set and costume designing, Tod had left the Yale School of Fine Arts to come west. It is through his eyes we see the people whom he felt he had to paint. At first he knew little about them except that "they had come to California to die." But as this "very complicated young man" wanders amid the sets and costumes of the real Hollywood, the painting takes shape in his mind. Each fragment, a little more terrifying than the last, falls into place. As prophet-artist he plans "The Burning of Los Angeles" to show the flames like "bright flags." Los Angeles will have a "gala air" as it burns. The people who set it on fire will be a "holiday crowd." As prophet he sees more than a single city gone mad. Angelenos may be the "cream" of America's madmen, and their city may be the first to be consumed in flame, but "their comrades all over the country would follow. There would be civil war." Amid a screaming tidal wave of humanity—a crowd turned "demoniac"—Tod imagines what his painting will show when finished. His vision becomes the fact; his dream of doom, doom itself. Tod, who from the first has made every effort to remain detached and objective, is at the end broken in both body and mind. With his leg fractured by the mob, he is lifted into a police car, its siren only a little louder than his own hysterical scream.

West said that this novel showed "the peculiar half-world" of Hollywood.[11] Randall Reid speculates that the force in this half-world resembles a Freudian "revolt of a mass id against those 'higher' powers which have denied it and tricked it"; or a Marxian "outrage of victims who have been cynically exploited by a system"; or a Nietzschean "revenge of Dionysian frenzy against a fraudulent Apollonian dream."[12] More striking than these suggestions is what D. H. Lawrence called the "inner diabolism" below the surface of American life, or what Melville called the "power of blackness." It is a power only the greatest American writers have probed. It is a power of tragedy, that fateful nemesis which, to prove its agency, destroys the dreamer.

West shows a power of violence beneath Hollywood's facade, a surging force not to be placated by swimming pools, fast cars and movie premieres, and emphatically not by Hollywood's bizarre cults. Throughout all of West's novels this ominous force lies under the surface, breaking out in Balso's dream of murder; in *Miss Lonelyhearts* it is the violence accompanying the sacrament, or stories of gang rape, or Miss Lonelyhearts' own violence against an old man sitting on the toilet cover who refused to tell his life story like another Brokenhearted or Sick-of-it-all. American success-at-any-price accounts for much of the violence in *A Cool Million*. In *The Day of the Locust* violence and prophecies of violence shatter nearly every scene. In a short piece entitled "Some Notes on Violence," written in 1932 when West joined William Carlos Williams in editing the little magazine *Contact*, he observed that "almost every manuscript we receive has violence for its core." The manuscripts came "from every state in the Union, from every type of environment, yet their highest common denominator is violence." "In America," West wrote, "violence is idiomatic."[13] In his own novels there is that peculiarly American penchant for what in *Miss Lonelyhearts* West calls an "orgy of stone breaking." Beneath the physical acts of violence West probes for reasons (which become evident in *The Day of the Locust*) why Americans have smashed their cultural heritage. Rather than merely sloughing off their Old-World traditions, they have rebelled against them; they have smashed them, much in the manner of Rölvaag's *Peder Victorious*. With desperation they seek a new order.

The new order is the frontier and, inevitably, Southern California. As with Miss Lonelyhearts, who developed "an almost insane sensitiveness to order," Americans who saved their dollars and rejected their heritage journeyed west to the land of sunshine and oranges, accepting the desperate wager to unite with this order celebrated by cultists like Maybelle Loomis, the "raw-foodist" and follower of character Dr. Pierce, whose motto was "Know-All Pierce-All."

One such American in West's last novel is Homer Simpson, whom Tod recognized as "an exact model" for the westward bound. Homer had worked for years as a hotel bookkeeper in Wayneville, Iowa. He had saved his money and had migrated to California for his health. Homer's life in Iowa had been "without variety or excitement," a life of "totaling figures and making entries." Vulnerable as he is to the Hollywood dream befitting his name, Homer instead is stunned by the crazy, violent half-world represented especially by Harry Greener and his daughter Faye. Moreover, Homer confronts his own emptiness, his constantly trembling hands signaling the existential panic he feels within himself. Knowing his "anguish is basic," he thinks of yet other frontiers—of Mexico "only a few hundred miles away" or of the boats leaving daily for Hawaii. Unlike Faye, who has the wild energy for violence, and unlike Harry Greener, who can laugh a horrible, "machinelike-screech," Homer can only cry and, in the end, coil fetus-like on his bed, an escape far better, thinks Tod, than Religion, Art or South Sea Islands.

Homer's "Uterine Flight" as an alternative to the acceptance of life contrasts with that other alternative—violence. Both lead to self-destruction, but it is the destruction of society that preoccupies West, the kind of anarchic energy that impels the mob to have its own blood. Having dreamed the great dream and found it fraudulent, having gone to California and found even the sun a joke, the people feed on violence. With nothing else to titillate their ennui, they devour the newspapers and movies, the endless suppliers of sex crimes, explosions, murder and war. Yet this fare is not sufficient, for theirs is a deeper sickness than boredom. Not only do they feel cheated but, more importantly, they feel lost. They no longer know who or where they are, so successful has been their masquerading and so monstrous are their phony Swiss chalets, Mediterranean villas, Egyptian temples and Mexican ranch houses. Their anonymity breeds fear and their fear breeds hate. These are the dark powers too voracious to be satisfied by cock fights or a staged Waterloo.

The final scene of the novel is like nothing else in American literature, unless it be Hawthorne's "Earth's Holocaust," a story set on the western prairie, where an Emersonian philosopher tends a giant fire intended to consume "the weight of dead men's thoughts." Whatever is associated with the weight of tradition—books, trappings of religion, monarchies, inventions—and impedes human progress towards a utopia of spirituality fuels the reformer's holocaust. What stays untouched is "that foul cavern" the human heart. "Purify that inward sphere," Hawthorne writes, "and the many shapes of evil that haunt the outward, and which now seem almost our only realities, will turn to shadowy phantoms, and vanish of their own accord." Hawthorne, however, expected no such millennium, for what he saw lying in that dark cavern was human pride. Nathanael West likewise envisioned no millennium, and he too perceived that lying more deeply than fear and hate is pride—the pride that leads to war abroad and, when the locusts turn on each other, to Waterloo at home. The Waterloo this time is not on some collapsing Hollywood set.

What West sees is the collapsing American myth of the open frontier, the tragedy of a society too proud to accept the disparity between promises and realities. It is in no way ironic that one of Miss Lonelyhearts' detractors should utter what may be the final truth in West's fiction, and the final significance of its journey theme: "we have no outer life, only an inner one, and that by necessity."

9

The West and Eschatology

SOMETHING ESCHATOLOGICAL is in the unfor-
gettable scene that opens William Faulkner's *Light in August*.
For four weeks Lena Grove, far along in pregnancy, has been
journeying westward from her home in Alabama, searching
for her lover, Lucas Burch, who has reneged on his promise to
return. As she asks for his whereabouts, all the while with
"unflagging and tranquil faith," her journey becomes "a long
monotonous succession of peaceful and undeviating changes
from day to dark and dark to day again," and the many wagons
she rides in are "like something moving forever and without
progress across an urn." The unhurried miles nevertheless un-
roll, and Lena draws ever closer to fictional Jefferson (Mississippi), where, on the day she sees it from the crest of the final
hill, two columns of smoke rise. One comes from a coal stack,
the other from a burning house where Joanna Burden lies
murdered, her neck so deeply slashed that her head faces back-
wards. The smoke Lena sees from the distant hill portends the
violence she will know once she leaves the pristine world behind her and enters civilized Jefferson. Smoke and fire signal
the journey's end. They also forebode that "last ding-dong of
doom" in that "last red and dying evening."[1]

Whether or not man prevails—and Faulkner insists he
will—the concern with last things dominates Nathanael West's
The Day of the Locust, and is epitomized in Tod Hackett's
painting, "The Burning of Los Angeles." Other American
titles evoke this same fascination: books like William Styron's
Set This House on Fire and James Baldwin's *The Fire Next Time*.
One thinks of the climactic burning in Henry James' *The Spoils
of Poynton* or Hawthorne's story "Earth's Holocaust" as well as
Ethan Brand's final words: "Come deadly element of Fire. . . .

Embrace me, as I do thee!" As between fire and ice, Robert Frost wryly resolves the eschatological question by joining "with those who favor fire."

"What will America do—," asks Perry Miller, "what *can* America do—with an implacable prophesy that there is a point in time beyond which the very concept of a future becomes meaningless?"[2] This prophesy is Christian eschatology, brought to America by the Puritans who pondered The Book of Revelation and the words of Jesus in the Gospel according to Luke: "I am come to send fire on the earth"; Puritans who had probably read again and again that line from John Donne's Holy Sonnet (Number 7): "All whom the flood did, and fire shall o'erthrow"; and the same Puritans who later knew Milton's *Paradise Lost*, especially its direful Books Two and Three. Even though they sought the fulfillment of a New Jerusalem, their vision necessarily committed them to a fiery apocalypse. This literal conflagration had nothing to do with America as such. Puritan poet Michael Wigglesworth's "The Day of Doom" described a universal fire given frighteningly local context in Increase Mather's sermon, "The Day of Trouble Is Near." For all his spatial imagery the far more sophisticated thinker Jonathan Edwards made the apocalypse something internal. His "Sinners in the Hands of an Angry God" describes an all-consuming hell of despair engulfing "the foolish children of men [who] miserably delude themselves in their own schemes, and in confidence in their own strength and wisdom." Emblazoned though its imagery is, Edwards' prophesy failed to sway eighteenth-century Americans who saw nothing cataclysmic about to befall an already perfect order in nature and a perfectible order in the mind. By the next century the notion of an attainable paradise discounted the prerequisite fire and brimstone. In the popular acceptance of unlimited progress, eschatology was irrelevant. Expansion westward put to rest anxieties about either fire or ice. The infinite frontier made the Christian prophesy seem absurd.

The question Perry Miller asked stems from what to an American is an even more fundamental question: "Can an errand, even an errand into the wilderness, be run indefinitely?" Originally the errand was to establish a Biblical polity, a holy commonwealth in all matters both civil and ecclesiastical. Later generations, filtering out the moral severity in this covenant, made the errand into something more social, economic, even utopian. Confident in their strength and ingenuity, they easily filtered from their doctrine the human condition of sin. By the nineteenth century the utopian dream was far more American than Christian, primarily because eschatology had been expunged from it. Melville might describe the Galapagos Islands as once the scene of a great "penal conflagration," but the overtones bore no relation either to the American or to what had become the edenic wilderness. The open frontier was the perfect symbol for the American utopia.

This is why Frederick Jackson Turner's 1893 announcement carries such shattering implications. Not only does it destroy the nineteenth-century American Dream, but it brings back into the American consciousness what for two centuries had been denied. In those fateful words—"the frontier has gone"—concluding his famous essay, Turner revived the eschatological question upon which the Puritans had looked with both dread and fascination. To speculate about last things is to accept the possibility of limitation. To accept this possibility is to contemplate the end of the long American journey and to discover, with shocking abruptness, that, as inheritors of Puritan theology, we have been commited to this end from the beginning.

One way to interpret T. S. Eliot's line in *Four Quartets*—"In the end is my beginning"—is to suggest that we begin to come of age when we end illusions of infinite possibilities. But only initially is this Eliot's point; his was a Christian position, one that committed him not only to human limitation but to divine salvation as well. This is what Christian eschatology finally means: fire is itself a judgment, and from this judgment will come a new heaven and a new earth. American tragedy stops short of this vision. To prevail is hardly to say we will know the millennium. What we know is the closed frontier and the likelihood of worse things to follow. Thinking about Hiroshima, Perry Miller concludes his book on the Puritans' errand into the wilderness with the haunting reminder that "catastrophe, by and for itself, is not enough." He could have said that tragedy is not enough. Miller said he was "too wise" for such speculation, daring not to tread the silent country beyond tragedy. However, Montana's Norman Maclean glimpsed it, seeing where his father walked—where, as a "fool" amid impossible possibilities, he heard the Word that has its origin beyond the water and the stars.

II

Eleven years before the nineteenth century ended, Mark Twain published *A Connecticut Yankee in King Arthur's Court*, and seven years into the new century Henry Adams privately published *The Education of Henry Adams*. Both of these important books make explicit what Frederick Jackson Turner only implied, if, indeed, he was conscious of the eschatological implication that his 1893 essay carried. But the force of this theme in Twain and Adams enforces their conviction that the end of the century marked the *eschata* of history. They both foresaw catastrophe of national if not cosmic proportions. The apocalypse in Nathanael West's *The Day of the Locust* validates what had been seen half a century earlier.

Culminating in an Armageddon, *A Connecticut Yankee* does not concern the triumph of modern technology over medieval feudalism as much as it damns this same technology. The novel is less about the conflict of two civilizations as it is about American civilization itself, with the technology of destruction its hallmark. The real theme of the book is totally American; its structure, as Henry Nash Smith, a Twain scholar, points out, brings into conflict two cultural symbols—the American Adam and the American Prometheus. Hank Morgan, functioning as Mark Twain's Yankee, supposedly retains the American democratic ideals fostered by an earlier frontier society, even though he is the superintendent of the Colt Arms factory in Hartford, Connecticut. In the novel he begins more as a representative of those agrarian values idealized by Cooper and Whitman than as someone transformed by closed, urban industrialism. But this was exactly Twain's problem. Could an Adam become a Prometheus? Could humane individualism function in a technological society? Could a Natty Bumppo run one of Andrew Carnegie's steel mills? Twain's answer is visualized in imagery of Armageddon. It was an answer costing Twain unspeakable anguish, for he had earlier believed in the American ideal of illimitable progress. At the time he questioned this ideal, he wrote *A Connecticut Yankee,* and the work created "a crisis so severe," writes Professor Smith, "that it led to an almost complete loss of control over his materials."[3] Nevertheless, his answer was fixed, and in what was to be his last major novel Twain made clear that Adam had indeed become a Promethean monster, an extension of the machine and all its nonhuman imperatives. As if to prove to the rest of the world that American common sense and technology must triumph, and that those people sitting in darkness be considered simply as the common enemy, Hank Morgan, the American Prometheus, carries out his errand with dynamite and Gatling guns, the nineteenth-century equivalent to napalm and nuclear missiles.

But Morgan as The Boss does not conquer, even with twenty-five thousand enemy corpses around him. Disguised as a peasant woman who escaped the carnage, Merlin emerges to confirm what "Clarence," in the novel's postscript, already knows. Morgan and his fifty-three men are in a trap of their own making. If they stay in their defenses, the poisonous air bred by the surrounding mountains of dead will kill them. If they leave their fortifications, they will no longer be invincible. Like a Greek chorus pronouncing final doom, Merlin entones, "Ye were conquerors; ye are conquered."[4] He prophesies that all the transformed Connecticut Yankees will die, except The Boss, whom Merlin puts to sleep for thirteen centuries to reawaken in the late nineteenth century as testimony of total alienation from his edenic heritage.

Twain saw that American democracy, at one time nurtured by frontier ideals, was now being changed into something inhuman and grotesque. The depth of his despair is indicated in the novel's last chapter, "The Battle of the Sand-Belt," a description of flawless killing that only modern technology can accomplish. With the efficiency of a computer, The Boss merely presses buttons to detonate hidden land mines that reduce thousands of the enemy to "homogeneous protoplasm with alloys of iron and buttons." At the precise moment when thousands more advance among electrified wire fences, The Boss shoots current through all the fences, striking "the whole host dead in their tracks! *There* was a groan you could *hear!* It voiced the death pang of eleven thousand men." The remainder—"perhaps ten thousand strong"—faced the Gatlings that "began to vomit death" into them. In back the knights were trapped by a moat engineered to fill instantly. Halted by the "deluge of fire" in front, the enemy broke, turned about and "swept toward the ditch like chaff before a gale." Ten minutes completed the annihilation.

Reading through what Twain wrote in his last years explains why Bernard DeVoto, in discussing this period, called his essay "The Symbols of Despair."[5] Not only was Twain stricken with personal and financial tragedy, but questions about the nature of reality haunted him like a nightmare. Such stories as *The Mysterious Stranger*, "The Great Dark," "Which Was the Dream?" and "Which Was It?" supply his own frightful answers to questions he raises in his excoriating treatise *What Is Man?* (1904). Throughout these works a tone of impending disaster makes life and reality dreamlike. "Nothing exists," says Satan in his final speech in *The Mysterious Stranger*, "save empty space—and you."

> It is true, that which I [Satan] have revealed to you; there is no God, no universe, no human race, no earthly life, no heaven, no hell. It is all a dream—a grotesque and foolish dream. Nothing exists but you. And you are but a *thought*—a vagrant thought, a useless thought, a homeless thought, wandering forlorn among the empty eternities!

Of the many "symbols of despair" in Twain's late work, the burning of his family home occurred in both "Which Was the Dream?" and "Which Was It?" In two narrative fragments—"The Passenger's Story" and "The Enchanted Sea-Wilderness"—a burning ship served as an alternate symbol. The symbol of apocalyptic destruction stems from 1895 when Twain revisited his old Hartford house where he had lived during his seventeen most productive years. He imagined the event, according to John S. Tuckey, as a "homecoming fantasy," one in which he found himself "still at home with his family."[6] But his loss of fortune and, in 1896, of his daughter Susy to fatal meningitis served notice that his dream house was disastrously ruined. More than a symbol of disaster, it was for Twain a symbol of despair, suggesting the end of everything. His nightmare was, in fact, his life.

That Twain yearned for a home forever lost but never forgotten compares with the way he faced his own contemporary America. Under the crusading banner of imperialism, this America was not only the instrument of death abroad but, thoroughly deluded, the destroyer of its own frontier ideals at home. In the mass slaughter that ends *A Connecticut Yankee* and in the cold rationality that accomplishes it, Twain's own fear, says Professor Smith, "seems categorical and primal." For Twain rationality itself had become "a secularized version of Original Sin, and no means of redemption [was] in sight."[7] On this fateful conclusion, Mark Twain rested his case against America.

III

What was violence in Mark Twain's eschatology was entropy in Henry Adams' thinking. Twain's vision was of destruction, either an Armageddon with corpses piled mountain high or a home burned to ashes. For Adams the chaos was silence, the inexorable dissipation of energy until, like a comet in the night sky, civilization disappears into the zero of darkness colder than ice.

Broadly read in nineteenth-century science, Adams appropriated the second law of thermodynamics to fashion his eschatology. This law, made famous in the 1850s by the English physicist William Thomson (or Lord Kelvin), states that mechanical energy in the material world is dissipating at such a rate that within a finite time the earth will be uninhabitable. Contrary to Newtonian physics, this law denies the conservation of energy. Variously called the law of dissipation, the law of entropy, the law of degradation, it posits inevitable catastrophe as its central point. Its claims led astronomers to announce the death of the solar system, physicists the death of the sun, geologists the death of the earth, and anthropologists the death of the human race. In an effort to burst the superficial optimism of his own generation, Adams summarized the positions held by these nineteenth-century scientists. In his "Letter to American Teachers of History" (1910) he quoted the geologist M. J. de Morgan who asserted in 1909 that "the cold will return," that with the coming of glaciers populations will be pushed back into ever-smaller areas until, finding no more space, they "will be driven to internecine destruction." Even more portentous was his quoted announcement of M. Camille Flammarion, a noted astronomer, who described the time when "the last tribe, already expiring in cold and hunger, shall camp on the shores of the last sea in the rays of a pale sun which will henceforward illumine an earth that is only a wandering tomb, turning around a useless light and a barren heat." The second law of thermodynamics provides no escape. As a form of what Adams called "Vital Energy," man is "convicted of being a Vertebrate, a Mammal, a Monodelphe, a Primate." His flesh and blood condemn him to destruction— "science has shut and barred every known exit."[8]

Furthermore, Adams insisted that social energy was governed by the same law as physical energy. The historian, therefore, was as much a scientist as was the physicist. As such, Adams worked through one hypothesis after another to account for order and system in human affairs. Most notable are his essay, "The Rule of Phase Applied to History" (1909) and such chapters as "The Grammar of Science," "A Dynamic Theory of History," and "A Law of Acceleration" in *The Education of Henry Adams*. What he passionately sought was some kind of synthesis, some all-embracing law to unify twentieth-century multiplicity. On the other hand, the giant dynamos he saw at the Chicago Exposition in 1893 convinced him that energy was chaotic. Symbolic of some awful and destructive power, they left him with a "terror"[9] that compelled him to search for an inviolable order. What Adams found as the central principle governing both the material and social world was nothing more than the principle of catastrophe.

The Education is the story of that foredoomed quest. More than autobiography, the book is exactly what he called it: "A Study of Twentieth-Century Multiplicity."[10] Its immediate correlative is his own loss of faith in a singular order of existence. The values he inherited, while not directly attributable to the frontier, were based upon a moral order promising both human and social perfection. Such a moral law, he said, prepared him more for the year one than for the new century. *The Education* traces a lost traveler seeking meaning in a world stretching far beyond his powers of comprehension.

Another correlative was America itself, especially its seething, post-Civil War capital of plotting politicians. The scandalous corner in gold organized by stock gamblers Jay Gould and Jim Fisk, the madness of Charles Sumner in proposing the acquisition of Canada by the United States, the political character of President Ulysses S. Grant (who was "archaic and should have lived in a cave and worn skins"), and the lesser corruption everywhere left Adams with no ideology to support. A traveler lost in his own country, he witnessed "the degradation of the democratic dogma," the title Brooks Adams gave to the 1919 book that contained his brother's three essays—"The Tendency of History," "The Rule of Phase Applied to History," and "A Letter to American Teachers of History." In Washington, D.C., was ample evidence for Adams to conclude that the second law of thermodynamics applied to American political life. The end indeed seemed in sight. The fateful year 1893, when Turner announced the end of the frontier and when Adams saw the dynamos in Chicago, was also the year Adams read with much interest his brother Brooks' manuscript, *The Law of Civilization and Decay* (published in 1895). Both eschatology and history were fast becoming synonymous.

The substance most important in *The Education* is Adams'

eschatological view of history. Throughout he was extraordinarily successful in sustaining dichotomies—mind and matter, chaos and order, unity and diversity, youth and age, winter and summer. But his artful synthesis ironically calls attention to the fact that any other synthesis except the one foreboding entropy and death was not for Adams to have. The book depicts the failure of Adams, the protagonist, to achieve a vision of unity all people dream of. In his "A Letter to American Teachers of History" he called this dream "the most deceptive of all the innumerable illusions of the mind"; as an idea it "survives the idea of God or of Universe; it is innate and intuitive." In *The Education* (one of America's great literary tragedies), Adams, the dreamer, confronts the inevitability of last things. Not only does he discover that "chaos was the law of nature" and order "the dream of man," he also finds the mind "looking blankly into the void of death." The inexorable processes of history take one to this final and inevitable end. The frontier is closed. Even the mind offers no escape. One's vital energies, like those of the universe, decline and die. Failure to transcend this destiny must necessarily be total failure. Literary theorist R. P. Blackmur calls Adams' failure "genuine." Intended as a glowing tribute to greatness, Blackmur writes that this kind of failure "comes hard and slow, and, as in a tragedy, is only fully realized at the end."[11]

IV

Even the briefest survey of nineteenth-century American literature indicates that the cosmic optimism of Emerson, Thoreau and Whitman did not carry the day. Emerson in "Circles" asserted that the soul knows no boundary, that "the heart refuses to be imprisoned," and that "there is no outside, no inclosing wall, no circumference to us." Edgar Allen Poe described in *Eureka* the annihilation of the universe and the entropy of mind. Thoreau, who understood the art of walking as something holy—a Saunterer was a Holy-Lander—took his direction westward where, he says in "Walking," he can go as a free man. In this direction "the nation is moving," and, he adds, "mankind progresses from east to west." Hawthorne, on the other hand, regarded flight, whether east or west, as delusion; in *The House of the Seven Gables* this wisdom is Hepzibah's when, pausing with Clifford on their brief but exhilarating train ride, she kneels on the station platform and prays to God: "Have mercy on us!" Whitman, the third member of the Romantic American triad, wrote Emerson a letter with a complimentary copy of his new testament, *Leaves of Grass:* "Master, I am a man who has perfect faith. Master, we have not come through centuries, caste, heroisms, fables, to halt in this land today."[12] By contrast, walls meant everything to Melville: walls enclosing Bartleby and Pierre, walls along the terrible Liverpool streets, chapel walls in which were masoned memorial tablets with black borders, and the most terrifying wall—the whale's head, a "dead, blind wall."

By the end of the century these clashing ideas took extravagant forms. On one hand, determinists saw life as nothing more than a mechanical problem. With such terms as "natural selection," "biochemical processes," "conditioned reflex," and "Archaeozoic Age," they created a world view founded on an unyielding mechanical determinism. Their authorities were Charles Darwin and Thomas Henry Huxley, Auguste Comte and Herbert Spencer, Ivan Pavlov and Sigmund Freud, Sir Francis Galton and Sir James Frazer. The outcome in American literature was *Maggie* (1893), *McTeague* (1899), and *Sister Carrie* (1900).

On the other hand, the New Thought movement, growing out from the Neo-Hegelians in St. Louis and certain Far Eastern mystics, claimed that the naturalistic world of physical force only hid the real world of mind and spirit. This movement led to Christian Science and the widespread popularity of Theosophy, Spiritualism, other occult groups and psychical research. Early inquirers included Orestes Brownson and Margaret Fuller. As the century waned, many more American writers were asking if cosmic consciousness was indeed the new frontier. Oliver Wendell Holmes in *Elsie Venner* (1861), Edward Bellamy in *Looking Backward* (1880), and William Dean Howells in *The Undiscovered Country* (1880), *The Shadow of a*

Dream (1890), and *Questionable Shapes* (1903), were all concerned with occult transcendence. To many Americans, Eastern mysticism and more specifically, Buddhism, offered the answer to a closed, determinist world. Percival Lowell wrote *The Soul of the Far East* (1888); John LaFarge, who traveled to the South Seas and Japan with Henry Adams in 1890, wrote *An Artist's Letters from Japan* (1897); William Sturgis Bigelow, *Buddhism and Immortality* (1908); Lafcadio Hearn, a long series of volumes about Japan where he had exiled himself.

The metaphor of the frontier relates to these conflicting, perhaps extreme ideas. An open frontier came to mean a new existence, a rebirth, enabling anyone to transcend space and time, mortality and death. Intimations of this new level of existence were supposedly evident to persons who had freed themselves from a materialistic or entropic world view. The whole New Thought movement, endeavoring to explain divine essence and its force in human affairs, sought a new species of man. As perhaps to be expected, it was to California that Annie Besant, successor to Madame Blavatsky as international head of the Theosophical Society, went in 1926 to supervise the newly gathered members of this new species in the name of Theosophy.

Most sensational of New Thought efforts to cross the metaphoric frontier was the investigation of extrasensory capacities. In *Forty Years of Psychic Research* (1936) and *The Mystery of the Buried Crosses: A Narrative of Psychic Exploration* (1939) Hamlin Garland documented his longtime psychical interests, which had begun when he wrote *Tyranny of the Dark* (1905) and *The Shadow World* (1908). Higher consciousness, telepathy, precognition, spiritualism all include the belief that a person can make contact with distant events or with supraphenomena by a process not involving sight, hearing, touch, taste or smell. Such miraculous inventions as the telephone and telegraph encouraged people's curiosities about thought transmission, especially between the living and the dead. Thomas A. Edison tried to make "a sort of valve" to allow "personalities in another existence" to have a "better opportunity to express themselves than the tilting tables and raps and ouija boards and mediums and other crude methods now purported to be the only means of communication."[13] In 1919, the year before Edison had announced his invention, Francis Grierson devised a "psycho-phone" to use during his lectures to the Toronto Theosophical Society. This "phone," supposedly effecting intercourse between this world and the next, brought messages that Grierson recorded in *Psycho-Phone Messages* (1921). Garland boasted that Los Angeles mediums whom he knew had received messages from the spirits of Henry James, Sir Arthur Conan Doyle, Walt Whitman and others. Edith Ellis in *Open the Door* (1935) reported contact with Madame Blavatsky, Abraham Lincoln, the Virgin Mary and Jesus Christ!

One way of escaping nineteenth-century conventions was to go west, another way was to go "beyond." Nothing was too eccentric and bizarre to keep the frontiers open. Americans hungered more for becoming than for being. They heard the irresistible words spoken by the serpent to Adam and Eve: "Ye shall be as gods!" The closed frontier, however, mocks such efforts to reach beyond the grave. Abruptly it confronts one with the essentials of *this* life.

These are harsh conditions for a nation whose myths allow no place for failure and whose foreign policy since the eighteenth century has been influenced by frontierism. In the present century frontierism has influenced American action at Versailles, Yalta and Nuremburg. A militant innocence was behind what J. William Fulbright labeled "arrogance of power." "Once imbued with the idea of mission," he wrote, "a great nation easily assumes that it has the means as well as the duty to do God's will." Unfortunately, arrogance rejects a sense of limitations, even though, as Fulbright said, history makes it clear that the world has endured all it can of crusading, "high-minded men bent on the regeneration of the human race."[14] The difference between contemplating God and playing God is a lesson that fills literature and history.

Santayana once observed that the American has never had "to face the trials of Job." What would his attitude be, Santayana wondered, "if serious and irremediable tribulation ever overtook him."[15] Perhaps the answer is Nathanael West's uncanny vision of the burning of Los Angeles, its violence signaling that of today's urban nightmare in which the tribulation and response are one and the same. Yet out from such self-destruction some persons still ask Job's agonizing question: "why is light given to a man whose way is hid, and whom God hath hedged in?"

10

Regionalism as Frontier Synthesis

IN looking first at the open frontier and then the closed, we find ourselves caught in the familiar Hegelian dialectic between one interpretation and its opposite, both subject to fault. It would be convenient to understand the two metaphors of open and closed in terms of mere sequence, one associated with the beginning of the nineteenth century and the other with the end. But the present-day situation respects the claims of each as represented in apotheosis and eschatology. The voices of Gary Snyder and Nathanael West still compel our attention. It was Hegel who argued that only through synthesis can opposing claims be reconciled and a higher level of truth attained. Accordingly, successive stages follow in which the synthesis becomes a new thesis countered by its inevitable antithesis from which, again, a still newer synthesis is reached. What Hegel perceived was a final monism, the Hegelian Absolute, in which the opposites, seen finally as illusory, give way to the unity of life, mind and God—a monistic idealism.

Such a synthesis may satisfy the person caught between opposites, between a restless back and forth which desires reconciliation. Between such awesome dualities as man and God, death and life, finite and infinite, confinement and freedom, actuality and vision, America's Concord philosophers seemed to have achieved such a transcendent, reconciling unity. Thoreau reverenced both the savage impulse to devour a woodchuck raw and the instinct to reach higher, spiritual life, but he makes clear that the "higher principles" induce purity of soul and finally one's upward "flow" to God. From the "facts" of animal life we realize a change, Emerson said, and "reappear" in a new and "higher" spiritual identity. Newness of being brought newness of sight, enabling Thoreau even on dark nights to see some "dull uncertain blundering purpose," and Emerson to turn the world to glass and see "all things in their right series and procession." As for Whitman, he sent forth his "barbaric yawp" to proclaim life not as chaos and death but "form, union, plan—it's eternal life—it is Happiness."[1]

To which philosopher William James is said to have replied, "Damn the Absolute!" We live, after all, amid the hum and buzz of culture, the jangle of national conflicts, and the threat of universal nuclear fire. We may gamble on transcendence but in more sober moments recognize it as a form of twentieth-century blackmail and those practicing it are guilty of what Jean-Paul Sartre called bad faith. Similarly, in identifying transcendence as philosophical suicide Albert Camus insisted that nothing assures us that this world is ours. The best we can hope for are "privileged" moments and places, not a single essence holding all things together but an infinite number of essences giving meaning to an infinite number of these isolated moments and places, made "privileged" only by a human consciousness that illuminates them by paying attention to them.[2] Consciousness suspends them in experience. From this epistemological starting point Soren Kierkegaard spent a lifetime refuting Hegel, and D. H. Lawrence mocked America's penchant for philosophical idealism including its Western apotheosis.

It is instructive to look to Lawrence's *Studies in Classic American Literature* (1922) with its opening chapter ("The Spirit of Place") in which he chides believers in transcendence whether as idealists or western visionaries. The impulse behind each is the "frenzy" to get away from life's dualities and gain the freedom to fulfill dreams of oneness in the West. "Henceforth be masterless" is what Americans want to be told, which is neither freedom nor wholeness.

Men are free when they are in a living homeland, not when they are straying and breaking away. Men are free when they are obeying some deep, inward voice of religious belief. Obeying from within. Men are free when they belong to a living, organic, *believing* community, active in fulfilling some unfulfilled, perhaps unrealized purpose. Not when they are escaping to some wild west. The most unfree souls go west, and shout of freedom.[3]

Real freedom answers what Lawrence calls a person's "deepest self." This self wishes for wholeness born not from reasoned thought but from the human spirit and its dark necessity to realize itself through the experience of body and place.

Lawrence sees the immense engendering that a sense of place makes possible for persons seeking self-discovery. Suggested here is not a particular place having mystical power that only the initiated or converted experience. It is not a shrine, mosque, temple, altar or "holy" city. In truth it may not be a place at all, at least not one on a map. Melville said that true places never are the ones cartographers show. The frontier synthesis is a sense of place that combines geography and the human spirit. This sense may be a shared experience made communal through myth and ritual and transformed into something timeless. But it permits no surrender of personality, no philosophical escape. On the contrary, even while open to mythical dimensions, a sense of place roots a person in history and locality. It makes experience the proof of truth. It demands coping with the exigencies within a closed and finite world.

The experience of place quickens awareness of others who walked the same fields or of a beloved person who built this house or planted that garden. The experience enlivens a sense of perpetual expectancy. In new places (the New World) come discoveries of old truths and promises of further revelations. Past, present and future unite to transform a place into an event. From such recognition comes the security of a human and fixed abode (perhaps a sense of *terra patria*) but more through intimate experience than collective egotism and pride. Having a sense of place may come as sudden epiphany or more likely a slow unfolding that permits one to grasp the significance of place only years later when we savor the encounter—

the farm, neighborhood, stream, hills, tree in whose branches we shared childhood secrets with a friend; savor it without its former intensity but with the glow of what has since transpired. A sense of place may be a "clearing" like a Robert Frost poem that generates delight at first and ends in a clarification of life.

What it means to experience this kind of synthesis goes beyond geography and words. New Englander Hayden Carruth, for example, has said that he read the "compendious and dismal" volumes by Van Wyck Brooks and his fellow critics, and the "compendious and perhaps less dismal" volumes by scholars in the thousands, but found no distillation to corroborate his sense of being a New Englander; no synthesis that matched "what I feel in my nerve and bone."[4] Wendell Berry answers to similar feelings about being a Kentuckian. The same can be said for the Muirs, Abbeys, Stegners, Graveses and Haig-Browns of the West. For each the hills are different. What for one person is the wet, green-black forest of fir and cedar is for another the jagged-edged Wyoming Rockies, the Arizona desert, or the low, rolling prairies. Each place is different, each has its distinguishing geography, but each also has a tallying human consciousness. Uniqueness is what makes all regions alike, and the human response is what unites us as brethren.

A sense of place means ontological orientation. Something primal is at issue, a primitive consciousness requiring that the place where we live connect with something axial (*axis mundi*). Our sense of being requires this corresponding sense of place. We call such a place home. It is an abiding and sheltering place without which we drift willy-nilly toward spiritual annihilation. D. H. Lawrence was right: we are free only so long as we obey the spirit of place. To disregard it is synonymous with a disregard for the sacred, and the consequence is a diminished self.

Voices from the past remind us that place is a metaphor for humanness. To sever a people from their ancient place is proof enough of inhumanity. An Indian voice says, "This is our home. . . . We cannot live anywhere else. We were born here and our fathers are buried here. . . . If we cannot live here, we want to go into the mountains and die."[5] When we have our homes, we are whole; without them we are nothing. Deep within the American consciousness these voices tell us that the place we claim as home was once the consecrated place of someone else. Our humanity is tested by the humility and sense of stewardship that our home engenders. We tread lightly, knowing that our inheritance will someday be our legacy to someone else. Thus, to know a place well is to know its context, and that context is ultimately the world, both the past and the future. Only with this degree of humanity can we hear the voice of someone like Chief Seattle who, in surrendering the land on which the city is now situated, said to an uncomprehending Governor Isaac Stevens in 1855:

When the last Red Man shall have perished, and the memory of my tribe shall have become a myth among the white man, these shores will swarm with the invisible dead of my tribe, and when your childrens' children think themselves alone in the field, the store, the shop, or in the silence of the pathless woods, they will not be alone. . . . At night when the streets of your cities and villages are silent and you think them deserted, they will throng with the returning hosts that once filled them and still love this beautiful land. The White man will never be alone.[6]

In recent years Western writers like Edward Abbey, Barry Lopez, Gretel Ehrlich, William Kittredge and Ann Zwinger— to name but five—have extended their nature prose into the social, political and psychological consequences that occur when modern technology threatens or destroys forests, tundra, canyons, rivers and ancient artifacts. With urgency and often despair they describe the erosion of soil and pollution of air and water. More nostalgically than other writers, Wendell Berry ruminates on the constant care required to keep a place a home. Such effort he calls "national defense," waged not by armies but people who, with a "particularizing passion," have always loved "their *homes*, their daily lives and their daily bread"—not their country in some abstract nationalist

patriotism.[7] Our greatest danger, he argues, is hollow patri-
otic passion and what he sees as its inevitable expression in
nuclear warheads. But the machines, chemicals and other "la-
bor-savers" are already to blame for environmental catastro-
phes as well as the displacement of people from agriculture.
The technologies of agribusiness enable less than three percent
of our people to keep the land in production, but these same
technologies do not and cannot enable farmers to take care of
the land. Vandalism is not only the littered streets and the
defaced and ruined buildings we see in cities, it is rural property gathered into too few hands and the shift of emphasis
from maintenance to production. It is also suburban "development" by "a powerful class of itinerant professional vandals"
who have no local allegiances, no local point of view—vandalism by a class that is both elitist and intellectual.[8] In the end
it is an economy driven by greed.

Greed breeds violence, symptomatic of prideful arrogance
and absolute ownership devoid of commensurate responsibility. Greed enables a person to desecrate a place, then leave it
and forget it, to take from it with no thought of restoration,
and, most poisonously, to destroy one's own sense of reverence. Something akin to a tragic sense colors Berry's thoughts
about an alienated people who hear no voices and feel no
reverence. "A people as a whole can learn good care only by
long experience of living and working, learning and remembering, in the same places generation after generation, experiencing and correcting the results of bad care, and enjoying
the benefits of good care."[9]

Whether it's too late to find meaning in such sentiments
does not negate their inherent good sense. Perhaps some remain who heed admonishments and find that the good life
includes being humble and grateful. The argument supporting
a frontier synthesis strongly insists that the good life needs a
sense of place. This synthesis rejects transcendence as well as
cynicism born of greed or existential anxiety. It dispenses with
self-delusion with its excesses of hope and imagination, and it
repudiates mere aestheticism that denies nature its numinous
aura and all too often encourages indifference toward suffering

and deprivation of others. Yi-Fu Tuan, the noted geographer, calls this combination of sentiment and place "topophilia" and describes it in numerous ways: fleeting visual pleasure, sensual delight, fondness of place because of familiarity, among others.[10]

Yi-Fu Tuan also includes vertical meanings which have pre-occupied the psychologist of religion Rudolf Otto, the anthropologist Mircea Eliade, the mythologist Joseph Campbell, the literary critic Northrop Frye, the historian Frederick Turner, the theologian Jurgen Moltmann and many more. Geographer Tuan, firmly holding to his horizontal metes and bounds, identifies vertical dimension as being charged with sacredness. Granted that by the seventeenth century the vertical of the medieval world had begun to yield to the horizontal, and that with the secular displacement came the loss of awe and holiness. Yet Tuan, the scientist, affirms that when seen through the "eye of caritas," or charity,[11] nature affords a significance to the dispossessed not unlike the significance of home to the wanderer or water to the thirsty.

II

The key that unlocks the multiple definitions of regionalism is *caritas*. The true regionalist who loves his home knows it as a metaphor for wholeness, centeredness and connection. It is there he finds clarification and the good life.

Our concern is the literary regionalist, the artist who feels in his nerve and bone what it means to be a Westerner, a Texan, an Oregonian. The artist feels because he merges his own experience of place with the people and events that have come before, and with the fuller symbolism into which they have expanded. The artist recapitulates all these things within his psychic depths. Events, themes and people grow to become part of him as their creator. It is accurate to say that he possesses them rather than controls them. Indeed, the place may possess him. What emerges is the artist's voice, as complex and universal as the human condition. Both the artist and the region come alive through the transforming power of imagination, spirit and love. Person and place are wedded each to each. The game of art becomes the game of grace, and as participants the readers recognize the miracle.

When seen developmentally, the first stage of regional literature includes letters, diaries, journals and papers of all sorts—in short, a written record through the eyes of newcomers that gives a time and a place to geography, to settlement, to the original inhabitants and to affairs of the immediate day and season. The second stage reflects an effort to understand the raw details of the first. The second-generation historian, for example, arranges records to support an interpretive thesis, or he gains one by such arrangement. Whichever way he proceeds, he seeks to understand the primary materials he now controls. The artist at this stage does the same, although imagination infuses and shapes his understanding. Not having traveled the actual Oregon Trail does not prevent his using records to create his own Oregon Trail and peopling the wagons according to his interpretation and imagination. Sometimes he is guilty of misrepresentation. Other times he succeeds in stark and accurate verisimilitude. In this second level the writer identifies the larger themes that bind events together: the culture clash between whites and Indians, for example; the excitement of discovery and the strenuous work of pioneering and settlement; topography and the plenitude of nature; the use and misuse of natural resources; the rivalries among non-Indian ethnic groups and among social and economic classes. The writer also builds his characters according to roles prescribed by the boundaries of their ethnic, familial, occupational and geographic communities.

A third, culminating stage takes nothing away from the keen observation and acute sensibility that is necessary to interpret the first two.[12] In both levels the point is place; writers emphasize the adjective in the term "regional literature." In the third stage the accent falls on the noun. Stage three presupposes an artistic achievement joining artist and place, each bringing life to the other, each partaking in life as the common and universal denominator. Such an achievement testifies to a genuine frontier synthesis. "All events and experiences are local, somewhere," writes Oregon poet William Stafford, and all the arts "are regional in the sense that they derive from immediate relation to felt life . . . the stuff of the world."[13] Stafford suggests that locality is experience universally shared. Thus, Mark Twain's Mississippi River becomes part of everyone. The reader lives in Faulkner's Yoknapatawpha County, in Dickens' London and on Melville's whaling ship because the reader shares life with the artist, the consciousness of each modulating together. The artist's search for place is the reader's, the one's alienation the other's nightmare, and the one's assimilation the other's joy.

Something happens when a talented artist or writer captures the feeling for place. We sense authenticity, a truth of pattern and energy inherent in the object but distilled, intensified, shocking us into recognition. To echo Emerson's essay on "The Poet," the true regionalist possesses—and is possessed by—the woods and the river, the market and the mountains; others are only transients—visitors and tourists—ranging here and there without commitment. To the true regionalist—the person whose sense of place unites him to its underlying power—place becomes home, place touches the world's axis and thereby is made sacred. This is the meaning of roots: having a psychic relationship with place; knowing that something of yourself is in it and it in you.

To sever this relationship is to alienate oneself from the deep sources of identity. Enmity develops toward what surrounds one, and making war upon it follows. We vandalize, pollute, plunder and ravage what is separate from us; we revere, protect and cherish what we belong to. Separated we match our ego against the "other"—whether it be the land, the community or another human being—and in destroying the "other" we measure our triumph. By contrast, when we join with the "not me," the "Thou," we overcome our enmity and feel the same currents flowing through ourselves as through all living things. To destroy the "other" somehow diminishes us, like breaking a covenant with a friend. Something disintegrates within us. Spiritless, we look upon the world as only an "It." The "Thou" departs; the wrecking ball has no tears to shed.

Neither does the chain saw, the belching stack, the flush of toxic waste, or the person whose roots have shriveled, whose relationships have withered away and whose isolated heart feeds on nothing but its own self-hatred.

We might think of a tree the way the central character does in Don Berry's novel *Trask*. Trask has not only survived his *tamanawas* ordeal but has been "scoured clean" by it, and now as in a trance remembers that on his return to the Killamook village a giant fir had blocked his path and he had scratched and torn at the bark in rage until his hands bled. Suddenly he had heard the voice of dead Charley, once his Indian guide, say, "This tree wishes you no harm. Go around it in peace. You are hurting yourself. . . . You kill yourself."[14] Trask knew then that the tree was himself.

Nothing in Northwest fictional literature catches this sense of oneness with place better than the works of Ivan Doig, James Welch and Norman Maclean. In Maclean's novella, *A River Runs Through It*, the Big Blackfoot River of Montana is no less a presence than is the narrator who returns to the river and hears in it the long-lost voices of his brother and father, now dead. Words issue from the primal flood and the basement of time. "I am haunted by waters,"[15] says the narrator, speaking as one through whom his Montana river runs as it did in the beginning, does now and ever shall. This is what the frontier synthesis as regionalism is all about.

The Northwest's greatest regionalist poet is Theodore Roethke who literarily came of age in Seattle where he lived his last fifteen years. No mere tenant or tourist, he came as a pilgrim to the seashore and the rain forest, finding something of himself amid the barnacled rocks and oozing moss, and sharing the delirium of birds that wheeled around the hawthorn tree in his own garden. "There are those to whom place is unimportant," he wrote in his poem "The Rose," but for himself the place "where sea and fresh water meet" had special meaning. He lived "with the rocks, their weeds/ Their filmy fringes of green," with kelp beds and the "wind-warped" madronas. Among these things he came upon himself, as if "another man appeared out of the depths" of his being. His later poetry pulses with what he calls a "steady storm of correspondences" ("In a Dark Time") in which he meets himself in deepening shade and hears his voice in the echoing woods. "Leaves, leaves, lean forth and tell me what I am," he wrote ("The Sequel"). The I-It dichotomy is overcome; opposites merge into the oneness of Thou; and Roethke, a true regionalist, can say, "God bless the roots!... The right thing happens to the happy man" ("The Right Thing").[16] For Roethke the Northwest had become the source of poetic truth; even more, as essayist Kermit Vanderbilt puts it, "Roethke and his Northwest had finally come to One."[17]

The third stage of creation is internal assimilation and its associated joy. The irony at this level is that we find ourselves returning in a prelapsarian way to where we started from. We recognize that the most profound regionalists were the persons who were here long before we arrived with our axes and plows, diaries and journals. If only dimly, we are aware that the Indians knew what it was to live on holy ground, to have their ageless roots in it and to be in relationship with all that surrounded them. Moreover, their hallowed land was made more hallowed by the graves of their ancestors who, said Chief Seattle, continue invisibly to inhabit the shore and pathless woods and to be heard from within the waters. A writer like Roethke realized that in the radically alien vision of the original inhabitants he shared a heartfelt knowledge. He knew a sense of place and gained truth from it.[18]

11

Three Montana Regionalists

IVAN DOIG, JAMES WELCH,
NORMAN MACLEAN

For some persons a better term than "sense of place" may be "privilege of place," suggesting what Albert Camus had in mind when he identified "privileged" moments of existential clarification associated with the sun-blazed sands of Algiers. For our best American regionalists the term "power of place" serves even more tellingly. Something happens that makes one place different from another, makes responses different, makes words different. For Ivan Doig, Montana has a power to summon, grip and possess him, and he must answer or in some way understand it. At times he seems pursued by this power, other times pursuing it. Either way, remembering is his epistemological groundwork, bringing forth what he calls "a set of sagas we live by."[1] Remembering is knowing and knowing is ordering; memories seek understanding and understanding comes through patterns and patterns through words. In composing words he composes himself but in relation to place. In remembering Montana he quickens to the power that the place evokes and to the urgent need to answer or obey it.

Of the several books that Doig has written, *This House of Sky* best dramatizes the regionalist's mind in action. He resurrects place and answers it. His memory brings Montana to Seattle, where he presently lives, and brings the past into the present. His Pacific Northwest days, he confesses, "would seem blank, unlit, if these familiar surges could not come." When they do, a certain turn of his desk chair becomes the creak, "the quick dry groan of a saddle under my legs—and my father's and his father's." The present is the past and *vice versa* when memories of Montana mountain weather, "this skewed rhythm of the year," call to mind the Pacific coastal waves that "comb in before me this minute." A face from his Montana grade school twines with one met "a week ago on a rain-forest trail in the Olympic mountains." When fixing a sandwich lunch he finds himself sitting down thirty years ago in the company of an old cowboy. Moreover, "I glance higher for some hint of the [Seattle] weather, and the [window] square of air broadens and broadens to become the blue expanse over Montana rangeland . . . a single great house of sky." "How thin the brainwalls must be," he ruminates, how close to our present consciousness must be the random people of the past. Indeed, the past rises to meet the present, fuses with it, and the "brainwalls" dissolve. Whatever explains this phenomenon—whether epiphany, some powerful imaginative moment, a privileged connection and clarification when the spirit of place bridges barriers of miles and years—Doig's *This House of Sky* becomes a kind of epistemological textbook that records his way of knowing.

In a bold stroke the author composes seven glosses, one appearing at the end of every chapter. Each is a memory sketch, a kind of mythic essay that reveals contours of Doig's western mind; each serves as a vertebra in the deeply structured spine that integrates the book. The first three pieces probe beginnings—the earliest moments in the childhood mind, when we see our parents as "tribal gods" and our hidden selves as "marauders [and] marauded, too." One might wish Doig had expanded on this thought, but the point must certainly be to suggest the paradox of the young searcher already being the one sought by some inchoate but greater power. More clearly, that power which he first associates with Montana he will recognize later as death. Also thematic in these three sketches are the emergent life patterns made by his remembered instants. Indeed, the book's central metaphor is that of pattern, so uneven at first, "so gapped and rutted and plunging and soaring," and at the end so endurably fixed even amid personal loss.

The metaphor of "noon" is described in the fourth gloss

that accompanies the book's pivotal chapter, "The Lady." In this midway chapter the focus of the book becomes clear. Both Charlie and Ivan (father and son) have been profoundly emptied by the death of Ivan's mother Bernata Doig, then embittered by the divorce of Charlie and his second wife Ruth. By agreeing to join the bereft father-son household, Bessie Ringer, Bernata's mother, completes the triadic pattern, in Doig's words: "my father and my grandmother and myself"— three generations joined together—"a threesome-against-life." Bessie is the keystone, her coming the "noon" in the curve of the day from morning beginnings to evening endings.

In the fifth gloss Doig not only affirms this triad but aches to find words adequate to his blood. The "blood-words" are those he wants most to find, words having the power to texture this essential threesome with bright exact tones. In nerve, bone and blood he yearns for a "language of meaning" and "phrases of kinship." Although hardly groaning in travail, Doig seems almost biblically Pauline about this search for words, for he finds nothing easy or unafflicted in the struggle, and his house of sky has interceded with sighs too deep for words.

In the next gloss Doig tells a story out of memory, heard from his father "a hundred times, and never enough"—a story of Charlie's killing a "damned bear" that had kept coming into the ranch and killing sheep. But he could not hide the fact that he shook all night afterwards, after it was all over. In the repeated way Charlie had told the story, the son detected some "lilt of wonder" in his father's voice that he could have been "both hunted and hunter."

Being prey is the deeper truth and Doig explains that in the gloss to the final chapter "Endings." He tells of Charlie's death, Bessie's passing and, in the memory gloss, Ivan's "scuff" against death one afternoon on the Olympic Peninsula. Thrashed by the Pacific Ocean surf while being sucked into it, Doig awakened to "incredible clarity" as the feeling of death settled into him. As Ivan came whirling out of the surf one more time, a helpless onlooking friend later said he saw on Ivan's face "a look of deep resignation." The curve of the day,

which took father and grandmother to their endings, fore-
shadows the author's destiny and calls up in him the endings
put to the others. However, the triad holds fast. In life Ivan
shares with the departed Charlie Doig and Bessie Ringer "the
sensation of having been swirled out of deepest hazard."
Death notwithstanding, Ivan's links of memory tie the three
together.

These seven sketches take the reader down to where the
creative process begins. They record what Doig's memory offered up, not only in the rich detail texturing the chapters
themselves but in a mythic pattern of creation-preservation-
destruction, a configuration that he raises to the more explicit
higher level of *memory-pattern-death*.

First, memory with its immediacy provides the stuff of
Doig's direct consciousness and creative wellspring for the
subsequent rich flowering. Next, Doig's patterning comes in
the interlocking triads, the archetypal one consisting of Charlie, Bessie and Ivan, or what the author calls a "makeshift
family," an "edgy alliance of a household," "something-both-
more-and-less-than-a-family," a "knot of concern." As if part
of some psychic mandala, the family's emotional fabric evolved
out of similar feelings—anger, relief, gratitude—woven into
Doig's consciousness as he stands by his father's grave. This
pattern ties into still another—family, work, steadfastness—
personified in Bessie and integral to the human threesome in
which Ivan has his place. The generations-old pattern Charlie
inherited and passed on consists of "landscape, settler's patterns on it [and] the family fate within the pattern." Finally,
whereas death completes the mythic pattern and the more
immediate configuration of the book; and whereas death is
omnipresent throughout, linked to Ivan's first recollections
and to his final vision, death is not part of the triad that rules
This House of Sky.

The paramount reality comes from three living persons, and
it grows evermore steadfast and beautiful. Death only high-
lights life. Death is the stage upon which life is played, but the
play remains the thing. Death and skirmishes with death;
death that hunts down its victims while still in their young

years; the "siege of death-against-life" as in the painful mor-
phology of Charlie's dying; the White Sulphur Springs cemetery where Charlie Doig and Bessie Ringer lie side by side
with other Doigs and Ringers in a somber space not much
larger than a garden patch—but death is not the book's triumph. Life is. And its heartbeat is love. In the end the triumphant triadic pattern holds because—like the bond between
Charlie and Bessie, early seeded in armistice, alliance and acceptance—the pattern outgrows its own trellis and flourishes
first in affection and then in love.

As metaphor, the quilt Ivan's "Grandma" had been stitching
occupied the morning of her final day. It was "another of her
rainbow-paneled splendors." Before noon she phoned a friend
near Ringling, asking to be brought some fresh eggs. Soon
after, her son, Ivan's uncle, called to check on things. In the
afternoon she passed up a funeral of a friend but helped serve
coffee and chatted with the mourners. Supper she ate alone at
home. Later at the Senior Citizens Club she joined in the
weekly card party. In the midst of something joked, Grandma
slumped, chin onto chest. That was that. It was the end of a
splendored life that in its wondrous autumn colors had embraced both son-in-law and grandson.

The life pattern represented by the threesome is a hard-won
synthesis born from a series of attacks and defensive counter-
attacks. Nothing that survives comes easily in Doig's book. In
it death is the chief assailant. It is everywhere in the author's
memory including that moment soon before daybreak of his
sixth birthday when his mother's breathing grew more ragged,
then stopped. Asthma took her as emphysema later took his
father who, long before, had had nine brushes with death
(Doig recounts each). The close calls do not include a Mayo
Clinic stint fairly early on that cost Charlie two-thirds of his
stomach and for a while left him a bony ghost. Furthermore,
Doig relates the various endings that came to his Doig grand-
parents, his uncle Jim, Bessie's husband Tom Ringer (Ivan's
grandfather) and Mr. Magnusson for whom she cooked, and
Mrs. Tidyman in whose Valier High School English class Ivan
had first discovered realms of gold. If less definitive, no less

inexorable were the hardships of homesteading that Doig traces back; always the "belligerent" landscape of high-Montana rangeland, always the government practices allowing big ranchers to subdue the small, always the winters that "fought us again and again" and the corresponding landscape left frozen and empty.

"I know now," he writes, that such silences as those the Doigs and Ringers knew "came out of years of having no other defense." Reprieves proved heartless, resistance unavailing, as one by one the various homesteaders on their "stunted" ranches disappeared:

> . . . the McLaughlin place there by that butte, the Vinton place over this ridge, the Kuhnes place, the Catlin place, the Winters place, the McReynolds place, all the tens of dozens of sites where families lit in the valley or its rimming foothills, couldn't hold on, and drifted off. All of them epitaphed with the barest of words, *place.*

Against a nameless adversary—call it fate—the ranchers had stood their ground as best they could. Like that of the others, Bessie's defense was her steadfastness although it seemed to Ivan more than that. During Charlie's final illness she created doilies and tablecloths and those special quilts that seemed to Ivan almost to dance with colors, "snipped and-sewn diamonds of ragwork marching and playing and jostling like a meld of rainbows." And the impulse behind it all was "to push back against the grayness" settling over Charlie's ending days. As for Charlie, his defense had been his "heritage of perseverance," his "endurance of mind," enabling him to fight against the "grindstone" routine of ranching, the "mauling weather," and one calamity after another, all of which to Ivan seemed a "gauntlet." Long before escaping it by going to Northwestern University near Chicago, Ivan's earliest defenses had been the times of joy with his father—the two together—Charlie permitting his young son's company in the White Sulphur Springs bars and cafes: Stockman Bar, Melody Lane, The Maverick, The Grand Central, The Mint, Ham & Eggs, The Pioneer, The Rainbow. During the hard-edged boyhood years following his mother's death, Ivan sensed that by allowing him into this "blazing grownup world, with its diamonds of mirror and incense of talk" his father treated him as already grown. The two together, "the widower and his son, had begun to steady."

When father and son reached out to Bessie Ringer who, herself bereft, riveted their outreach to her own, the three together forged a defense that even fate could not destroy. Fired on the one hand by the adversity brought on by death, a turbulent second marriage and divorce, a child's loss of security and failures of homesteading, yet tempered on the other hand by an armistice that changed to love, the human bond hammered from the synthesis seemed all-sufficient. Yet something more was there, something present all around them that awaited their discovering eyes and hearts. Both Charlie and Bessie knew it most acutely in Chicago and later in Seattle where they felt so out of place. They knew their place was Montana.

As for Ivan, no matter that during his Montana youth he "hopscotched" from place to place. In the several years between his mother's death and his grandmother's arrival, he had followed his father through seven or eight places to live, and in the next year and a half he "ricocheted" among a half dozen more. No matter that after high school he left Montana for Northwestern University, then married and later moved to Seattle. No matter that he turned into the dusty furrows of scholarship that led him to a University of Washington Ph.D. in history and later to full-time freelance writing. Leaving Montana did not mean Montana left him. To the contrary, he found himself "veering inward," discovering himself to be more his father's son, and his grandmother's grandson, than he had ever known before. And more, in what must be the book's crowning testimony, he realized now, long years after their death, that his own "single outline meets the time-swept air that knew theirs." Certainly that air was the same that whistled down the Montana mountains and across the fertile ranges of his mind.

And what holds *This House of Sky* together? What does it

embody? We know that its sources were the deep Montana experiences that Doig remembered and his heart-filled imagination shaped. We also know that time is on the side of the book, and not that of its author. With his inevitable end the final segment of the triad will someday disappear. But sinewed into the book the patterned coda survives. Such is the wonder and irony of art.

II

Even though Ivan Doig depicts Montana's great upland ranges as landscapes of loneliness, hardships and hard-fought survival, his house of sky is not so vast as to nullify his interlocking patterns of human relationships. The patterns hold firm against the assaults of nature, fate and death itself. But Doig delineates little of the soul's anxiety should the patterns not hold and even less of the soul's forlornness. In the story, Ivan is not forsaken; his father Charlie sees to that, and his grandmother Bessie completes the security.

By contrast, the distances in James Welch's *Winter in the Blood* (1974) extend beyond Montana's sweeping horizons. Almost entirely psychological, these distances reach out to nothing, leaving the narrator of the novel disconnected, lost and abandoned in a world he never made. Whereas Doig's central metaphor bespeaks union, that of Welch suggests the opposite: an existential emptiness in which the narrator feels "no hatred, no love, no guilt, no conscience, nothing but a distance that had grown through the years."[2] Each character in the novel has known his or her own private world of distance, but for the unnamed narrator the distance, chiefly within himself, makes his need to find connections a matter of his soul's survival. Whereas Doig's book stems from the need to understand relationships existing from his childhood, and uses overt details of geography, history and autobiography, Welch's novel depicts a soul in despair and touches the much deeper levels of existential psychology and religion where winters were "always timeless and without detail." Only as the narrator can regain feelings of anger, love and conscience can he regain life; only as he rediscovers himself is there hope of reaching others.

Other contrasts between the two books exist. Most notably, epiphanies in *This House of Sky* come from the author's memory and his "scuff" against death miles away on Washington's Pacific Coast. Doig's insights come as something achieved years later, over morning coffee, or at his typewriter, or from occasional trips to the library. Epiphanies come to Welch's narrator, however, directly on his Montana homeland, amid the very cottonwoods that sheltered his Blackfoot people (including his grandfather and grandmother) long winters before. It is a place still alive with ghosts. Connections happen with the thrilling, sudden, powerful immediacy of the moment, yet only after the agony of his empty distances and the torment, both literal and symbolic, of his wounded knee. Welch's insights are seen as redemptive, life-restoring. For Doig, home is more a state of mind that memory weaves from long-past experiences; for his counterpart, home is a place sanctified by the truths spoken only there and no place else.

Welch's narrator is distanced from his beloved father, First Raise, and brother, Mose, both dead; from his mother, Teresa, and her second husband, Lame Bull; from his nearly blind and certainly toothless grandmother almost a century old who spends her final days in a squeaking rocking chair; from his Cree girlfriend Agnes; from his Indian heritage, as well as the tawdry white culture replacing it; from the natural landscape now polluted and desecrated; and finally from his own sense of self, home and centeredness. But the narrator comes to understand the distances that others "close" to him have also suffered. For the old hunter Yellow Calf the distance was the many years he spent as close as a three-mile path to the woman he loved, yet never lived with, their affair "so solemn and secretive it had not even been rumored." Now for the first time the narrator, lost in his own crisis, learns from Yellow Calf that the hunter had saved the old grandmother from starving during the terrible winter when she, beautiful and only twenty, had been ostracized by her struggling people.

They had thought her a curse when their leader Standing Bear, her husband, was brought back dead from a desperate raid on the Gros Ventres for food. As her only hunter, Yellow Calf had loved her secretly for years before Teresa was born and long years after. Yellow Calf's story completes the one told the narrator by his grandmother, and it also pieces together fragments told him by his mother Teresa and by his own instincts concerning that three-mile distance. For the first time he knows himself a true Blackfoot, not as some rumored, the grandson of the half-breed Doagie. He knows that his grandmother was the daughter of a chief and the wife of a chief.

He dimly remembers a snowy day as a child when his father took him to see Yellow Calf but said nothing to identify the old man as the boy's grandfather. The childhood journey serves the narrator in memory as an "event of distance"; he felt it then and feels it now but in a different way. This day Yellow Calf's words powerfully restore Welch's protagonist to the task at hand, and to what he must do "next time." As for the task at hand, his grandmother's death the day before means a grave has to be dug today for the burial tomorrow. At it, he later says, were "the four of us"—Teresa, Lame Bull, himself and his grandmother—each alone in ways both comic and pathetic, yet together at the tiny ranch graveyard where a Styrofoam cross marks First Raise's grave and a white wooden one, topped with a circle of Styrofoam, marks Mose's. Undistracted by Lame Bull's banal eulogy and Teresa's moaning, the grandson ponders silent thoughts of Agnes. Next time he finds her he would "do it right. Buy her a couple of cremes de menthe, maybe offer to marry her on the spot." Indeed, Yellow Calf had made him feel good to be home.

In this important regional novel Welch's motif embraces both "winter" and "blood." The former suggests the deaths and the seasons of despair visited upon the narrator, his family and his race; the latter evokes the stuff of life, often spilled but forever vital. Never mutually exclusive, the two metaphors merge into the synthesis of truth that makes one without the other something less than life. A sense of tragedy shadows life, but the shadows presuppose light (as lostness presupposes an axial centeredness, and despair, hope). Home is where Welch validates this truth.

The honesty that permeates the novel stems from Welch's profound understanding of this paradox. His narrator has returned from a far country. But even home as a mere place heals nothing until he joins heart-to-heart with someone else, either in love or truth or both. As for the homecoming, it was never easy, and now "it had become a torture," with his right eye swollen and his throat, head and bad knee aching in the heat of the day. He had come home to the burnt Montana prairie and a blazing sun, cracked gumbo flats, the polluted Milk River, sagebrush and dry cottonwoods—and to a mother, an old grandmother and a girl some thought was his wife. But "none of them counted," none meant anything to him. As for the girl, he had come home to learn she had left three days earlier. Such imagery portrays an Eliot wasteland, everything dry and empty, distances endless and all the myths gone.

Where the thirty-two-year-old wanderer has come *from* is left untold except for his mother's reference: "She [Agnes] left three days ago, just after you went to town." Whatever the town—the novel focuses upon Havre—Welch signifies "town" as a surrealistic correlative to the mythless land. For all the realism in depicting bars and flophouses, and the drunks who fight and fornicate and wander aimlessly, Welch shows his narrator as a stranger everywhere. Whether in the world of the "stalking white man" or that of the Indians who "were no bargain either," he was "a stranger to both" and both had beaten him.

Years earlier he had gone to Tacoma for a second operation on his knee. He had stayed two years to work in the rehabilitation clinic there. Even though well-liked because he was smarter than the others, he refused to play the showcase Indian hired so that the clinic could get grants. His bad knee no better, he left to barhop among Seattle's derelicts, and for ten years he had been in transit.

He marked time from the winter day neighbors had found his father frozen stiff in a gravel pit. He too had been a wanderer, never really leaving but never staying either. He would go to town—Dodson—and drink with the white men, who despite their mocking laughter respected his knack for fixing things, and who "gave more than his wife." After brother Mose was accidentally killed, First Raise stayed away longer, sometimes for a week or two. One day he stayed away forever. Whatever distance Mose's death had left the father with, the distance for the brother seemed infinite.

The searing memory of his brother's dying was as indelible as the ever-present pain in his knee. On a late autumn day when he was twelve and Mose fourteen, both were riding Bird. The horse bolted into an oncoming car. The narrator could never forget "the futile lurch of the car as the brake lights popped, the horse's shoulder caving before the fender, the horse spinning so that its rear end smashed into the door, [Mose] flying slowly over the top of the car to land with the hush of a stuffed doll." Our narrator had clung to the saddle horn, staying on until Bird jolted down the slope of the road's shoulder. The rider tumbled from the horse's back, down into "the dark weeds" where his knee struck something hard, a rock or a culvert. The knee injury and the horror of the moment had become one and the same, a psychic wound, the past a part of every present moment.

Of course the overtones extend to that other Wounded Knee in South Dakota, where at dawn on December 29, 1890, soldiers of the American Seventh Cavalry decimated the last of the Sioux, leaving them in frozen heaps to be collected later for burial in a common trench hacked out of frozen earth.[3]

Although a homecoming begins *Winter in the Blood*, the narrator's sense of home is suspended until near the end when Yellow Calf's story provides the healing epiphany the narrator needs to make home truly his. Without the necessary linkage the initial homecoming is cruelly ironic, with wastelands of mind and spirit stretching to infinity.

When he sets out for Havre to find Agnes (who refuses to return with him), he also finds, once again, the twentieth-century American nightmare that Welch's "town" represents. Havre is Nathanael West's Los Angeles in miniature where people are worse than they seem and yet nothing seems real. Enroute he stops first at Dodson, then at Malta where in the drunken miasma of Minough's bar he helps Agnes' brother Dougie roll a stranger but spies Dougie snatching the wallet for himself. The narrator gets the barmaid instead, awakening the next morning still gripped in the nighmare that had jumbled together the girl and Teresa and gutted fish, the duck Amos of his childhood, a mysterious airplane man and a host of leering men. His next stop is Harlem, Montana, and Malvina's perfumed bed.

Havre marks the final stop in this circle of hell, and Marlene's thighs a sudden vision of swarming tiger tails and blue dots, millions of them, and somewhere in the distance a muffled guitar accompanying someone singing "If you loved me. . . ." The guitar now thrums violently, followed by clatter like a chair being knocked over. Outside, the traffic roars. Inside, deep inside his crazy kaleidoscopic world, the women come and go: the Malta barmaid, Malvina in Harlem amid her bubble-bath globes and perfumes, and Agnes in her short blue dress, standing defiantly and helplessly on the sidewalk. Meantime, Marlene flails her legs, and when it's all over "he felt the kind of peace that comes over one when he is alone, when he no longer cares for warmth, or sunshine, or possessions, or even a woman's body, so yielding and powerful." A sense of anhedonia settles heavily upon him as he thinks of the enigmatic airplane man, Dougie's savage fist, Agnes' defiance, Marlene's limp body resembling "a bug floating motionless down an irrigation ditch"—and the stabbing pain his wounded knee brings up from the past.

After two days Welch's narrator has had "enough of Havre, enough of town . . . enough of the people, the bartenders, the bars, the cars, the hotels"—enough of hell, enough of himself. No clues in Havre will point him to himself, and no mirrors along its streets will tell him who he is. With residual impetus the wanderer finds the grit to walk away from Havre and not look back.

After his hitched ride drops him at the ranch, his true homecoming begins. Almost as if he were carrying out a ritual, he enters the kitchen and finds the tub in which he and Mose used to bathe. Then, the dirt was of a different kind, "dirt from the roads, chaff from the hayfields—not the invisible kind that coats a man who has been to town." He heats water. Because of his bad knee he cannot squat so hunches over to use the soapy washrag. He suspects his grandmother has died during the weekend because neither she, Teresa nor Lame Bull are around. Radio music fills the kitchen while he washes away the grime of "town."

Obeying some inner prompting, he saddles Bird the next day and takes the news of his grandmother's death to the old man Yellow Calf. Returning along the old three-mile path, he feels himself transformed by the news telling him who he is. Like a savior, Yellow Calf has given his grandson a history and in this sense has redeemed time. He has also given him a sense of authentic locality and thus has redeemed his place.

The third phase occurs when Bird and his rider, nearing the corral, hear a bawling calf and see its mother lying on her side, up to her chest in the muddy slough. "I wanted to ignore her . . . to let her drown in her own stupidity, attended only by clouds and the coming rain." As a psychological correlative to the enormous rebirth struggle raging within himself, he manages to extricate the cow, releasing a torrent of pent-up anger and spending his remaining physical strength and that of the white horse. From somewhere deep within himself, groaning in travail until now, he hears the "rumble of thunder, or maybe it was the rumble of energy, the rumble of guts." Out of the rumble and the cleansing rain comes a great awakening of spirit even as, at the same time, the colossal strain of the rope costs the pale horse its life. In the midst of the storm's rumble old Bird totters and goes down, but the rope attached to the saddle horn holds and the cow emerges from the ooze.

The narrator finds the inner strength to absolve Bird for having bolted into the car long years before. Whereas nothing seemed to matter after that, now everything matters to the person who is home and alive again. Later standing at his grandmother's grave, dug a tad too small for her coffin and requiring Lame Bull to jump up and down on its lid, the narrator resolves to see the doctor about his wounded knee, and next time to do it right with Agnes. Now even his grandmother's old tobacco pouch matters, and he tosses it into the grave.

In richly structured ways, *Winter in the Blood* recounts the homecoming of a nameless Indian man, a soul-wanderer, unfixed and uncentered, who regains a genuine sense of who he is only when he finds himself united with time and place, history and land.

III

Norman Maclean, the third Montana regionalist, makes religion an explicit component in his novella, *A River Runs Through It* (1976). Although sharing with Ivan Doig and James Welch a regional consciousness, best described as psychological (thus giving personal meaning to a sense of place), Maclean uses orthodox Christian theology to add typological dimension as well. To say this does not imply that Doig and Welch lack spiritual perceptiveness; Doig is broadly humanistic in his, Welch is tribal and cultural. But the challenge Maclean poses is a regional consciousness that combines Judeo-Christian and mythical perspectives, the one affirming a God of history and the other venerating a gentle paganism with its celebration of soil, fertility, vegetation and the seasons. Through these perspectives Maclean discerns places—specifically Montana's Big Blackfoot River—as charged with special sacredness. Moreover, he uses the New Testament concept of *caritas* to bring out this same quality in human beings. The river is not only a place where he once fished with his beloved father and brother, but a place where boredom, cynicism, anxiety and the world's horror give way to the transcendent magnificence toward which the river as both symbol and type flows.

Thus on a level that is only implicit in Welch and even less suggestive in Doig, Maclean addresses questions that twentieth-century literature asks with special urgency. Critic Lionel Trilling writes, "It asks us if we are content with ourselves, if we are saved or damned—more than anything else, our literature is concerned with salvation." Trilling cites such writers as Yeats and Eliot, Joyce, Proust and Kafka, Lawrence, Mann, and Gide. The point, says Trilling, is not that these writers are "actually religious," but that they manifest a "special intensity of concern with the spiritual life which Hegel noted when he spoke of the great modern phenomenon of the secularization of spirituality."[4] What Havre is for Welch, Helena is for Maclean—a world not only messy and corrupt but damned, totally secularized. The distance from this world to that of the Big Blackfoot River is the journey Maclean's narrator takes. For the author himself, an emeritus professor of English at the University of Chicago, the novella evokes the home he once left and has returned to.

"In our family, there was no clear line between religion and fly fishing."[5] The analogy Maclean creates in this arresting opening sentence takes on intriguing resonances that include the questions Trilling names, and leaves the reader sharing the feeling expressed in the novella's closing sentence: "I am haunted by waters."

Christ's disciples were fishermen, those on the Sea of Galilee were *fly* fishermen, and Maclean's favorite, John, had to be a *dry-fly* fisherman. This was the logic Maclean as a boy learned from his father's Presbyterian sermons. Yet for all the sermons preached and heard, and all the hours the boy and his brother Paul studied *The Westminster Shorter Catechism*, what really restored their souls, including that of their clergyman father, was to be in the western Montana hills where trout rivers run deep and fast. Ernest Hemingway had said in "Big Two-Hearted River" that swamp fishing was a "tragic adventure"; for Maclean, fishing the Big Blackfoot River was a redemptive one, thanks not only to divine grace but to self-discipline. The theology is sound Calvinism: God does all, man does all.

As for human nature, theologically speaking, just try to use a fly rod for the first time and, says the author, "you will soon find it factually and theologically true that man by nature is a damned mess." Again, Calvin couldn't have said it better. Only the "redeemed" know how to use it. Until such a time, a person "will always take a fly rod too far back, just as natural man always overswings with an ax or golf club and loses all his power somewhere in the air." Natural man does everything wrong; he has fallen from an original state of harmony. And he will continue to be a mess until through grace and discipline he learns to cast "Presbyterian-style." The great lesson the father taught his two sons was that "all good things—trout as well as eternal salvation—come by grace and grace comes by art and art does not come easy."

All this theological business is not as heavy-handed as it sounds. Indeed, Maclean transforms it into characterization, metaphor, humor and fine detail. He also transforms memories of his father and brother into Rembrandt portraiture edged in darkness and tragedy but also pervaded by the light of a haunting presence, a prelapsarian truth associated with sacred origins, the divine *logos*. Maclean would have us see fishing as a rite, an entry into "oceanic" meanings and eternities compressed into moments, epiphanous "spots of time," the *mysterium tremendum*. Entering the river to fish its dangerous waters is to fish eternity and to unite in love with those few persons who also obey the exacting code. None obeyed the code more religiously than brother Paul who, when entering the river, made fishing into a world perfect and apart, a place where joy comes first in a perfect cast, then in a strike that makes the magic "wand" jump convulsively, and finally in a big rainbow trout in the basket—in all, a performance of mastery and art.

Narrator Maclean remembers his brother Paul as a master dry-fly fisherman, indeed as a true artist when holding a four-and-a-half-ounce rod in his hand. But more, Paul was one for whom the river in its sacrality held answers to questions, and for whom fly fishing was the search for those answers. That, Paul said, was what fly fishing was, and "you can't catch fish if you don't dare go where they are." Paul dared, and he showed his brother and his Presbyterian father, both expert fishermen too, how to dare. On what was to be their last fishing trip together, before Paul's murder and the father's later death, all things seemed to come together—the river, the fishing, the father and two sons. Sinewing the union was love, and in the union the powerful Big Blackfoot River spoke to them. It is truly a redemptive moment, caught and held secure in Maclean's memory and in his narrative art. The story is equal to anything in Hemingway and a good deal more courageous theologically.

Support for this assertion needs to include Maclean's theological doctrine of man. Maclean says that man is a "damned mess." Maclean's courage comes not in asserting this doctrine, which Hemingway, Mark Twain and numberless other writers have had no trouble with, but in juxtaposing it with a doctrine of salvation. Without the juxtaposition, damnation is no less a bromide than is salvation. The courage comes in one's affirming a larger context of reality in which the juxtaposition both is and is not reconciled. To change the image, we might imagine a world where a river runs *through* it but is not *of* it. The test of courage is to embrace the paradox.

As for the messiness unto damnation, Maclean's story does not equivocate. The world is a fallen one, people are liars and cheats, family entanglements ruin the most blessed vision. When the narrator's brother-in-law steps off the train at Wolf Creek, we see Neal, genus *phonus bolonus*, dressed in white flannels, a red, white and blue V-necked sweater over a red, white and blue turtleneck sweater, and elegant black and white shoes. At Black Jack's Bar his big talk with oldtimers and the town whore, Old Rawhide, shows him in his true element. The family picnic the following day on the Elkhorn River shows him disgustingly out of it. He fishes not with flies but worms and gets nothing; he whimpers from his hangover and feigns sickness to avoid picnic chores. A genuine bastard, he deserves neither solicitude nor Montana. Neal violates everything that is good, including the code of fishing. On a subsequent trip he violates a trust by stealing beer that the brothers have left to cool in the river—and in *this* the Big Blackfoot River. Even worse, he has brought not only a coffee can of worms for bait but also Old Rawhide, and has "screwed" his whore on a sand bar in the middle of "our family river." The brothers find the two asleep, naked and sunburned. On the cheeks of her derriere they see the tattooed letters: LOVE. The river sanctuary has been defiled; never again will the brothers throw a line here at this hole.

Close as narrator Maclean appears to be to his brother Paul—both reverencing the river whose secrets only the best dry-fly fishermen can hope to touch—a vast gulf nevertheless separates them. If they both find the river an enigma where answers lie hidden in watery shadows, the narrator finds his brother an enigma as well.

That Paul seeks answers in fishing leaves his brother wondering about the questions being asked. Somewhere deep in Paul's shadowy inner world is chaos that the four-count rhythm of casting has not disciplined, a hell that grace has not transformed. Yet Paul seeks no help either from brother or father. Only the visible things show—namely, that he drinks and gambles and fights too much, that gambling debts translate into enemies, that his job as reporter on a Helena newspaper confirms a world full of bastards, and, finally, that he wants no help, asks for none, expects none except what the hard-driving river can bring. Clearly, Paul lives in a world more profoundly fallen than that represented even by Neal's damned messiness. Confirmation of this fact comes in the manner of Paul's death: beaten with the butt of a revolver, nearly all the bones of his right hand (his fighting hand) broken, and his body dumped in an alley—this, the death of a dry-fly fisherman whose rod was a wand of magical power and beauty, and who, when inhabiting this river-world, embodied laughter and discipline and joy.

Wherein, then, is saving grace? In the water? In the words that the father reads in his Greek New Testament? In the Word (the *logos*) from the Fourth Gospel that the father seeks to interpret as the two of them, father and son, wait on the riverbank to watch Paul catch his final big fish? "In the part I was reading," the father explains, "it says the Word was in the beginning, and that's right. I used to think water was first, but if you listen carefully you will hear that the words are underneath the water."

Now comes the crucial distinction.

"If you ask Paul," the son says, "he will tell you that the words are formed out of water."

"No," the father replies, "you are not listening carefully. The water runs over the words. Paul will tell you the same thing."

Of course, Paul never tells, and we suspect he has never found out. Neither his brother nor his father knows the truth about him. Yet the distinction deserves close attention together with the images that Maclean allows to arise from his memory, images that come out of the past to bear new meanings, joining the past and the present in the image and the image bearing the truth.

Watery images bring forth fish seen sometimes as "oceanic," with their black spots resembling crustaceans. The river itself flows from origins shaped by the ice age, the rocks by more elemental forces emanating "almost from the basement of the world and time." The rain is the same as "the ancient rain spattering on mud before it became rock . . . nearly a billion years ago." Whereas in the sunny world where the river-voice is "like a chatterbox, doing its best to be friendly," in the dark shadows where the river "was deep and engaged in profundities" and where it circled back on itself now and then "to say things over to be sure it had understood itself"—in these primal depths the voice issues from a "subterranean river" where only the most courageous ever venture and where only *real* fishing takes place.

Through such imagery Maclean takes us to foundations antecedent to water. From these foundations the father in the narrative hears words—words beneath the water, words before the water. The distinction between words formed out of water and words formed out of foundations beneath the water is the distinction between mystical pantheism and the Christian *logos*. The distinction is between the *unity* of creator and creation on one hand and their *separation* on the other. Again, the distinction is between the saving grace found in one's merging with nature, and that found in one's belonging to the God antecedent to nature, the God in nature but not of nature, immanent yet transcendent. And whatever the word spoken in the pantheistic unity, it is not the same as that spoken in the separateness, spoken in the *logos*, spoken from under and before the timeless rocks.

Maclean, the author, is involved in more than mere theological dialectic. What he is saying comes not from such abstractions but from memory and images, from time past when he and his father and brother were one in love if not in understanding. And now those he loved but did not understand are dead. "But," he adds, "I still reach out to them." Something of this love he still hears in the waters of the river and in the foundations beneath. Perhaps he hears the Word itself as did John of the Fourth Gospel. This is what his father must have heard too and what his brother Paul did not. Whether the words come from water or from the deeper foundations, they are words his memory translates into those of father and brother, words that spoke of love. In their words he has his epiphany, yes his redemption, and thus he can say, "I am haunted by waters."

Maclean's story is a classic, deserving a place in the pantheon not only of Montana but of American literature. Putting aside such matters as structure and tone, characterization, imagery and a hundred other elements that subtly harmonize (whether the art be that of Maclean's fiction or his fishing), one finds something else, something identifying the river as symbol and type.

As for symbol, all the age-old meanings associated with living waters—one immediately thinks of purification, fertility and renewed life—are predicated upon a perceiving mind and a symbolic mode of perception. The argument here concerns more the act of perception than the object, more the perceiver than the perceived or percept. In short, the perceiver as symbolist finds significance through the interaction of experience and imagination, whereas the perceiver as typologist finds significance through a sacred design that is prior to, greater than and independent of the self. The mode of perception makes all the difference, and in this analysis the two modes are radically different. Symbolism results in a direct interpretation of life, whereas typology relates to history, prophesy, teleology. The symbol is created in the womb of the perceiver's imagination, whereas the type is revealed within the perceiver's faith. Again, the symbolist possesses a special quality enabling him to fuse object and meaning; the typologist possesses a special but different quality allowing him to see what has already been fused and now revealed but is separate from and independent of him. Finally, the symbolist enters the river, as it were, and is redeemed by the waters which his imagination transforms into purification and renewal. But the typologist enters what has already been transformed or, more accurately, what flows from a sacred design, purpose, or destiny, made visible through the regenerate eyes and ears of faith.

In Maclean's story the two modes of perception show the river as both symbol and type. When attention is upon Paul's marvelous artistry, validating the halo of spray often enclosing him, we see by means of the narrator's imagination not only a transformed fisherman but a river metamorphosed into a world apart. Fishing becomes a world apart, a world perfect, an imagined and sinless world fusing person with vision. For Paul, when he steadied himself and began to cast, "the whole world turned to water." The narrator shares in the imagined oneness of his brother's world.

But the narrator does not lose himself in it. He also hears his father's words bespeaking a separate design, revealed as the *logos* or Word that was in the beginning—before the river and before human imaginings. More than speech, this Word is divine action—creating, revealing, redeeming. That the father carries his Greek New Testament along with his fishing rod is a fact not lost upon the author as narrator. Through his father's faith the son reaches out to hear this other Word. No wonder he is haunted by waters.

In truth, the Montana river runs through his mind and consciousness, language and life. But something also runs through the river itself, something that is in it but not of it, something more elemental than water. Call it the Word, the ultimate synthesis, where the abode of all passing things resides.

12

Home and the Good Life

CONCLUSION

THINKING about an open or a closed frontier triggers myriad symbolic meanings. "Open" invariably suggests freedom, hope, opportunity, perpetual youth, a second chance. Such symbolism intoxicates one's imagination, promising even such additional glories as rebirth, new sight and oneness with spiritual truth. Indeed, openness and apotheosis come together as one. No less suggestive is the term "closed," although the symbolic direction is opposite: limitation, fate, tragedy, age, and countless ramifications sometimes associated with maturity and wisdom, and at other times with despair and eschatology.

A problem arises when symbolism overshadows actuality. In becoming so bedazzled by symbol—especially when it unlocks worlds of psychology and religion—one may overlook the originating fact. America is a nation of laws, for example, even though its national symbolism triggers hope, glory and pride—attributes that can lead to tragic consequences. The point concerns the problem that occurs when the flag and vanity displace education in civics. This example does not nullify the importance of symbol and myth but speaks to the prior necessity for an awareness of fact and locale.

The problem is priority. When symbolists, triggered by the term "western" American literature, leap into action, they may nudge aside the fact of *place* implicit in the very term. Propensity to symbolize may eclipse the actual place, its people and the community's norms and visions, as well as the collective consciousness shaping them. Corrective attention directs one to the geography and the culture of place. A frontier synthesis returns symbol to original fact, and only then makes legitimate subsequent figurative links to something beyond.

The linkage is crucial and cannot be denied. Frontier synthesis is not mere literary realism. What the synthesis establishes is place linked to the reality of home. Clarification about who we are and where we belong come from such connections. Likewise, when a sense of place infuses a consciousness that recognizes its informing and nurturing origins are rooted in place, regional literature gains its identity.

Usually we think of place as something horizontal, something we can point to on a map or landscape and say, "There, that is my place." But a sense of place also includes something vertical. In Milton's *Paradise Lost* Raphael says in reply to Adam's question about "celestial Motions":

Heav'n is for thee too high
To know what passes there; be lowly wise:
Think only what concerns thee and thy being;
Dream not of other Worlds. . . . (VIII, lines 172-175)

Milton himself seems relieved to be "Standing on Earth": "More safe I sing with mortal voice" (VII, lines 23, 24). Nevertheless, the governing idea concerns the need to know where we are in the hierarchy, the vertical order of things—in the Great Chain of Being—in order to know our whereabouts in the horizontal, or the cultural and geographical. To recognize that the human place is neither with the gods above nor with the animals below is the need. To suppose otherwise is the sin of pride or atavism. In this sense everyone occupies the same "vertical" region, the same temporal and mortal place, where love, if it is to go on at all, will go on. Love is not likely to be sweeter elsewhere, neither in the idealized world of Southern California, nor the far reaches of transcendental apotheosis, nor down in the realist's barnyard. Knowing one's place in this hierarchical scheme is what Wendell Berry in his essay "Poetry and Place" calls knowing the "propriety" and then the "genius" of place—a matter first of decorum and then of an existential sense of what truly governs art and soul. On this point Berry deserves careful attention.

How you act *should* be determined, and the consequences of your acts *are* determined, by where you are. To know where you are (and whether or not that is where you should be) is at least as important as to know what you are doing, because in the moral (the ecological) sense you cannot know *what* until you know *where*. Not knowing where you are, you can make mistakes of the utmost seriousness: you can lose your soul or your soil, your life or your way home.[1]

Berry warns against isolation caused when one assumes to be elsewhere in the Chain of Being, either above the human lot through mind and idealization or beneath it in a state of primal wildness.

In the all-important relationship between the vertical and the horizontal, having a place in one establishes place in the other. As Berry puts it, "to be in place is good and to be out of place is evil, for where we are with respect to our place in the order of things and on earth is the definition of our whereabouts with respect to God and our fellow creatures."[2] A sense of place saves one from despair. At the same time it keeps one human, keeps one humble and keeps one connected to others within the horizontal. To disregard these things fosters dangerous rebellion, prideful individualism, anxiety and chaos— the tell-tale signs of unbridled frontier Romanticism. On the other hand, a sense of place keeps one in place. It preserves harmony with the surroundings, checks self-centeredness, tempers god-like imagination and inexorably assigns boundaries. Whereas symbol and myth carry one away into the abstract and the universal, a sense of place guarantees return. The birch tree bends and sets the climber down again. The higher the climb the more inexorable the return.

The antidote, if mortality itself is not enough, is the culture of place that regionalizes the universal, domesticates the wild, and establishes a community where each person, when connected with others, achieves a better freedom than what autonomy brings. Whatever we call this freedom, it is a means toward health whereas displacement and disconnection bring terrible malaise.

Of the many ways to describe this illness, surely its cause has to do with separation: the separation of mind and body, symbol and fact, life and locality, writer and region, words and feeling. The overwhelming symptom today is specialization. In his day Emerson described the specialist as a monster. "The state of society," he wrote in 1837, "is one in which the members have suffered amputation from the trunk, and strut about so many walking monsters,—a good finger, a neck, a stomach, an elbow, but never a man." Emerson added, "Man is thus metamorphosed into a thing, into many things" ("The American Scholar"). Our time is no different. Social mobility, corporate identity and trendy "lifestyles" mock tradition and sever connections based on history and place. Professionalism demands detachment and objectivity and justifies monstrous jargon. Critics and historians are no less guilty than engineers, politicians—even poets. In another of Wendell Berry's essays titled "The Specialization of Poetry," he deplores the specialist, this time the poet, who in lusting for selfhood renounces the world, breaks with the reader, repudiates tradition, preens "personality," and retreats into subjectivity that has no reference to other minds in the community, no connection to cultural memory, and no ties to earthly localities.[3]

The antidote is again culture, community, place, region, local habitation—concepts and landmarks that help save a soul and point one's way home. The best writers know this while the worst are full of passionate conceit.

It behooves one to know the difference by recognizing that conceit breeds a disregard for place. Ego sees every place as a projection of itself. Gazing at the gold doubloon that was cast with three Andes summits, topped by a flame, a tower and a crowing cock, Melville's Ahab boasted, "The firm tower, that is Ahab; the volcano, that is Ahab; the courageous, the undaunted, and victorious fowl, that, too, is Ahab; all are Ahab" (*Moby-Dick*, chapter 99). This is not connection but ownership, exclusion and deadly solipsism, all too translatable into what we see today: nationalism that spawns chauvinism that in turn brings on racism, fanaticism and madness and, in recognizing no boundaries, seeks to own more and more. Ahab loses his soul when he refuses Starbuck's plea to return home.

Home is not ownership. Home is where we share what we have. It is a place of mutuality, a place where we invest our sufferance and endurance for the sake of the communal soul. To be homebound is to be earthbound, and wisdom comes in devotion to the place that has nurtured us. Home is not a place we own but a place that owns us, not in mortgage but in nurture. Home is not property but placement.

What does home have to do with regional literature and specifically with western American literature? As for western, it is what its writers say the West has supplied them with or has given them. As with any region, the West gives what the writers have been open to receive. When Ivan Doig speaks of "atoms merging out of the landscapes into us,"[4] he is speaking for the true regionalist whether as writer, critic or local citizen. When Theodore Roethke says that he lived "with rocks, their weeds/Their filmy fringes of green,"[5] he is saying that others can live with them too.

Regionalism translates into a sense of place and *that* into a sense of home. Such feeling comes as an achievement. It may, of course, be a gift of grace like the inheritance of birth—some things we receive but do not choose or earn. But sensing real placement requires effort. We have the example of Twain returning to the long-lost river and discovering it different from the one he knew earlier; or Hemingway requiring displacement in order to know a real place, writing in Wyoming about Spain and in Paris about Michigan. We see Thoreau never leaving New England and Faulkner, despite his forays in Europe and Hollywood, never leaving the South, and both writers experiencing recognitions of place that awaken us to patterns in life, nature and divinity. Whether we cite these writers or Flannery O'Connor, Willa Cather, Sherwood Anderson, Wallace Stegner—or the Montana regionalists Doig, Welch, Maclean—we hear a voice that is believable because it comes from an authentic self, testifying to a hard-won union of person and place. Here is a real person who has taken the risk, allowing the patterns and energy of a place to touch and perhaps to possess him in such a way that he calls the place home. The discipline required for this union and for the force born from it involves both the felt life and the composed life. Feelings alone take us nowhere, but feelings composed and disciplined constitute what must be the good life.

Achieving a sense of home, like Shakespeare's "ripeness," acknowledges limitations but glories in the freedom that boundaries impose, and trusts the connections, both horizontal and vertical, that fix our place. Within such placement we dream the best dreams. What irony—this most popular myth of the West that heralds our independence from tradition, our ever-new beginnings and our limitless opportunities when, in fact, the very word "West" defines our region and roots us in it. For Westerners, the achievement is to see this wonderful irony.

Notes

Prospects, Limitations and a Sense of Place

1. T. S. Eliot, *The Family Reunion*, in *The Complete Poems and Plays, 1909-1950* (New York, 1952), p. 242.
2. Stephen E. Whicher (ed.), *Selections from Ralph Waldo Emerson* (Boston, 1960), p. 253.
3. Edwin Fussell, *Frontier: American Literature and the American West* (Princeton, New Jersey, 1965), pp. 285–291.
4. *Ibid.*, p. 394.
5. Northrop Frye, *The Educated Imagination* (Bloomington, Indiana, 1964), p. 55.

Frederick Jackson Turner: Frontier as Symbol

1. Unless otherwise noted, all quotations from Turner are taken from Ray Allen Billington (ed.) *Frontier and Section: Selected Essays of Frederick Jackson Turner* (Englewood Cliffs, New Jersey, 1961).
2. Benjamin W. F. Wright, Jr., "Political Institutions and the Frontier," in Dixon Ryan Fox (ed.), *Sources of Culture in the Middle West: Backgrounds versus Frontier* (New York, 1934), p. 16.
3. Merle Curti, *Probing Our Past* (New York, 1955), p. 32.
4. John C. Almack, "The Shibboleth of the Frontier," *The Historical Outlook*, XVI (May 1925), p. 197.
5. Wright, pp. 34–35.
6. A. O. Craven, "Frederick Jackson Turner," in William T. Hutchinson (ed.), *The Marcus W. Jernegan Essays in American Historiography* (New York, 1958), p. 264.
7. Henry Nash Smith, *Virgin Land: The American West as Symbol and Myth* (Cambridge, Massachusetts, 1950), p. 297.
8. Arthur M. Schlesinger, Jr., "The Historian as Artist," *Atlantic Monthly*, CCXII (July 1963), p. 38.

9. Carl L. Becker, *Everyman His Own Historian: Essays on History and Politics* (New York, 1935), pp. 191–232.

10. Fred J. Turner, "The Poet of the Future," *University [of Wisconsin] Press* (1883), pp. 4–6.

11. Smith, p. 298.

12. Louis M. Hacker, "Sections—or Classes?" *The Nation*, CXXXVII (July 26, 1933), p. 108.

13. Paul Tillich, *The Interpretation of History* (New York, 1936), p. 96.

The Tempered Romanticism of John Muir

1. John Muir, *The Story of My Boyhood and Youth* (Madison, Wisconsin, 1965), pp. 27, 63; William Frederick Badè, *The Life and Letters of John Muir*, 2 vols. (Boston, 1923), I, pp. 1, 19.

2. John Muir, *A Thousand-Mile Walk to the Gulf* (Boston, 1916), pp. 16, 30, 212.

3. Herbert F. Smith, *John Muir* (New York, 1965), p. 54.

4. John Muir, *My First Summer in the Sierra* (Boston, 1916), pp. 73, 146, 39, 250; Badè, I, pp. 218, 213.

5. Badè, I, p. 271; II, p. 31.

6. Badè, I, pp. 271, 21; Linnie Marsh Wolfe (ed.), *John of the Mountains: The Unpublished Journals of John Muir* (Boston, 1938), p. xvii; Badè, I, p. 325; Wolfe (ed.), p. xvii. For Muir's several letters to Emerson see Ralph L. Rusk (ed.), *The Letters of Ralph Waldo Emerson*, 6 vols. (New York, 1939), VI, pp. 154–157, 202–204.

7. Badè, II, pp. 28–29.

8. Wolfe (ed.), p. 95; Badè, II, pp. 7, 6, 117–118.

9. Badè, II, pp. 306, 317–318, 342–343; Wolfe (ed.), p. xvi.

10. Quoted references are to M.H. Abrams, *Natural Supernaturalism* (New York, 1971), pp. 69, 65.

11. Wolfe (ed.), p. 304.

12. John Muir, *Travels in Alaska* (Boston, 1915), p. 198.

13. Samuel Hall Young, *Alaska Days with John Muir* (New York, 1915), pp. 63–64.

14. John Muir, *The Cruise of the Corwin* (Boston, 1917), p. 109.

15. Wolfe (ed.), p. 191; Muir, *Letters to a Friend*, p. 81.

16. Badè, II, pp. 210, 211; Wolfe (ed.), pp. 337–338.

17. Lyon, p. 16; Wolfe (ed.), pp. 77, 89.

18. Badè, II, p. 279.

19. *Ibid.*, II, p. 354.

20. *Ibid.*, II, p. 364; Wolfe (ed.), p. 439.

The West as Apotheosis

1. Ray Allen Billington, *Frederick Jackson Turner: Historian, Scholar, Teacher* (New York, 1973), p. 454.

2. William Everson, *Archetype West: The Pacific Coast As A Literary Region* (Berkeley, California, 1976), p. 7.

3. For a survey of these interpretations see: Harvey Lewis Carter and Marcia Carpenter Spencer, "Stereotypes of the Mountain Man," *Western Historical Quarterly*, VI (January 1975), pp. 17–32. Also: William H. Goetzmann, "The Mountain Man as Jacksonian Man," *American Quarterly*, XV (Fall 1963), pp. 402–415; Don D. Walker, "The Mountain Man as Literary Hero," *Western American Literature*, I (Spring 1966), pp. 15–25; Max Westbrook, "The Practical Spirit: Sacrality and the American West," *Western American Literature*, III (Fall 1968), pp. 193–205.

The Closed Frontier and American Tragedy

1. Perry Miller, *Errand into the Wilderness* (Cambridge, Massachusetts, 1956); Charles L. Sanford, *The Quest for Paradise* (Urbana, Illinois, 1961), pp. 82–83.

2. R. W. B. Lewis, *The American Adam: Innocence, Tragedy, and Tradition in the Nineteenth Century* (Chicago, 1955), chap. 7.

3. Sanford, p. vi.

4. J. Frank Dobie, *The Longhorns* (Boston, 1941), pp. 41–42.

5. See Henry Nash Smith, *Virgin Land* (Cambridge, Massachusetts, 1950), chap. 16; Henry Steele Commager, *The American Mind* (New Haven, 1950), p. 41; Henry F. May, *The End of American Innocence* (New York, 1959); Van Wyck Brooks, *New England Indian Summer, 1865-1915* (New York, 1940); Leo Marx, *The Machine in the Garden: Technology and the Pastoral Ideal in America* (New York, 1964).

6. Mary Baker Eddy, *Science and Health with Key to the Scripture* (Boston, n.d.), p. 468.

7. Miguel de Unamuno, *Tragic Sense of Life*, trans. J. E. Crawford Flinch (New York, 1954), pp. 38–39.

8. George Santayana, *Winds of Doctrine* (New York, 1913), p. 191.

9. Max Wylie, "Aspects of E.G.O. (Eugene Gladstone O'Neill)," *The Carrell*, II (June 1961), pp. 1–12.

10. Daniel J. Boorstin, *The Image: or What Happened to the American Dream* (New York, 1962), p. 6; Allan Bloom, *The Closing of the American Mind* (New York, 1987); Carl Jung, *Modern Man in Search of a Soul* (New York, 1933), p. 108; Van Wyck Brooks, *America's Coming of Age* (New York, 1958), p. 78.

11. Joseph Wood Krutch, *The Modern Temper* (New York, 1929), chap. 5.

12. Arthur Miller, "Tragedy and the Common Man," in Robert W. Corrigan (ed.), *Tragedy: Vision and Form* (San Francisco, 1965), p. 150.

13. Reinhold Niebuhr, *The Nature and Destiny of Man*, 2 vols. (New York, 1941), I, p. 181.

14. William Faulkner, *Faulkner in the University*, eds., Frederick L. Gwynn and Joseph L. Blotner (New York, 1965), p. 26.

15. Joseph Campbell, *Hero with a Thousand Faces* (New York, 1956), p. 11.

Adventures of Huckleberry Finn: Barriers and Boundaries

1. Henry Nash Smith, *Mark Twain: The Development of a Writer* (Cambridge, Massachusetts, 1962), pp. 114, 124, 137.

2. T. S. Eliot, "Introduction," *Huckleberry Finn* (New York, 1950), pp. ix, xv; Richard Chase, *The American Novel and Its Tradition* (New York, 1957), pp. 148, 144; James M. Cox, "Remarks on the Sad Initiation of Huckleberry Finn," *Sewanee Review*, LXII (Summer 1954), p. 394; William C. Spengemann, *Mark Twain and the Backwoods Angel: The Matter of Innocence in the Works of Samuel L. Clemens* (Kent, Ohio, 1966), p. 131; W. R. Moses, "The Pattern of Evil in *Adventures of Huckleberry Finn*," *The Georgia Review*, XIII (Summer 1959), p. 166.

3. See Walter Blair, *Mark Twain & Huck Finn* (Berkeley, 1960), chaps. 11–13; also, Blair, "When Was Huckleberry Finn Written?" *American Literature*, XXX (March 1958), pp. 1–25. Regarding Twain's inconsiderate speech at John Greenleaf Whittier's seventieth birthday celebration (December 17, 1877), see Blair, pp. 155–158.

4. Leo Marx, "Mr. Eliot, Mr. Trilling, and Huckleberry Finn," *American Scholar*, XXII (Autumn 1953), p. 440.

5. Philip Young, *Ernest Hemingway* (New York, 1952), pp. 190–191.

6. Henry Nash Smith and William M. Gibson (eds.), *Mark Twain—Howells Letters*, 2 vols. (Cambridge, Massachusetts, 1960), I, pp. 91–92.

7. Quoted in Blair, p. 289.

8. Carlos Baker, *Hemingway: The Writer as Artist* (Princeton, New Jersey, 1963), pp. 180–181. Although Baker does not allege influence, he tellingly compares the prose opening chapter 19 of *Huckleberry Finn* and chapter 31 of *A Farewell to Arms*.

9. Karl Jaspers, *Tragedy Is Not Enough* (Boston, 1952), p. 42.

10. Northrop Frye, *Anatomy of Criticism* (Princeton, New Jersey, 1957), p. 213.

11. Albert Bigelow Paine (ed.), *Mark Twain's Notebook* (New York, 1935), p. 212.

Ole Rölvaag and the Immigrant Promise Denied

1. Ole Rölvaag, *Their Fathers' God*, trans. Trygve M. Ager (New York, 1931), pp. 234, 235.

2. Quoted in Theodore Jorgenson and Nora O. Solum, *Ole Edvart Rölvaag: A Biography* (New York, 1939), p. 26.

3. *Ibid.*, p. 167.

4. O. E. Rölvaag, "The Vikings of the Middle West," *American Magazine*, CVIII (October 1929), p. 47.

5. Ole Rölvaag, *Giants in the Earth: A Saga of the Prairies*, trans. Lincoln Colcord (New York, 1927), p. 111.

6. Percy H. Boynton, "O. E. Rölvaag and the Conquest of the Pioneer," *English Journal*, XVIII (September 1929), pp. 535–537.

7. Vernon Louis Parrington, "Editor's Introduction," *Giants in the Earth* (New York, 1929), p. xvii.

8. Henry Steele Commager, "The Literature of the Pioneer West," *Minnesota History*, VIII (March 1942), pp. 319, 326.

9. For a sustained analysis of Beret, see Harold P. Simonson, *Prairies Within: The Tragic Trilogy of Ole Rölvaag* (Seattle, 1987).

10. Ole Rölvaag, *Peder Victorious*, trans. Nora O. Solum (New York, 1929), p. 325.

11. George Santayana, *Interpretations of Poetry and Religion* (New York, 1957), p. 178.

12. Rölvaag to G. F. Newburger (October 22, 1931), Norwegian-American Historical Association, Northfield, Minnesota.

13. Jorgenson and Solum (eds.), pp. 265–266.
14. Quoted in Einar I. Haugen, "O. E. Rölvaag," *Norwegian-American Studies and Records*, VII (1933), p. 62.
15. Jorgenson and Solum, p. 323.
16. Ole Rölvaag, *Boat of Longing*, trans. Nora O. Solum (New York, 1933), p. 243.
17. Parrington, p. ix.
18. Jorgenson and Solum (eds.), pp. 155–156.
19. Rölvaag to Percy H. Boynton (June 3, 1929), Norwegian-American Historical Association, Northfield, Minnesota.

California, Nathanael West and the Journey's End

1. Quoted in Ray Allen Billington, *The Far Western Frontier* (New York, 1962), p. 149; Edmund Wilson, *The Boys in the Back Room: Notes on California Novelists* (San Francisco, 1941), p. 63.
2. Bayard Taylor, *Eldorado: or Adventures in the Path of Empire* (New York, 1949), p. 97; Billington, *America's Frontier Heritage* (New York, 1966), p. 26; Zane Grey, "Breaking Through: The Story of My Life," *The American Magazine*, XCVIII (July 1924), p. 80.
3. Franklin Walker, *A Literary History of Southern California* (Berkeley, 1950), p. 231; Zona Gale, *Frank Miller of Mission Inn* (New York, 1938).
4. Paul Jordan-Smith, "Los Angeles: Ballyhooers in Heaven," from Duncan Aikman (ed.), *The Taming of the Frontiers* (New York, 1925), pp. 285, 271, 279; *Religious Bodies: 1926* (Government Printing Office, 1930), pp. 457–459; *Los Angeles, a Guide to the City and Its Environs*, American Guide Series (New York, 1941), pp. 68–73.
5. James F. Light, *Nathanael West: An Interpretive Study* (Evanston, Illinois, 1961); Angel Flores, "Miss Lonelyhearts in the Haunted Castle," *Contempo*, III (July 25, 1933), p. 11; Victor Comerchero, *Nathanael West: The Ironic Prophet* (Seattle, 1967); Nathanael West, "Some Notes on Miss L.," *Contempo*, III (May 15, 1933), p. 2; Randall Reid, *The Fiction of Nathanael West: No Redeemer, No Promised Land* (Chicago, 1968), pp. 141–144; David D. Galloway, "Nathanael West's Dream Dump," *Critique: Studies in Modern Fiction*, VI (Winter 1963), pp. 60–61.
6. Quoted in Light, p. 69.
7. All subsequent references to West's novels are taken from *A Cool Million* and *The Dream Life of Balso Snell*, both novels in one

volume (New York, 1965); and *Miss Lonelyhearts* and *The Day of the Locust* both novels also in one volume (New York, 1962). The four novels are available in one volume, *The Complete Works of Nathanael West* (New York, 1957).

8. Herman Melville, *Pierre, or The Ambiguities* (New York, 1949), pp. 247–253.

9. Thomas M. Lorch, "West's Miss Lonelyhearts: Skepticism Mitigated?" *Renascence*, XVIII (Winter 1966), pp. 99–109; "Religion and Art in Miss Lonelyhearts," *Renascence*, XX (Autumn 1967), pp. 11–17; West, "Some Notes on Miss L.," p. 2.

10. Daniel Aaron, "Waiting for the Apocalypse," *The Hudson Review*, III (Winter 1951), p. 634.

11. West to Jack Conway, quoted in Richard Gehman's introduction to *The Day of the Locust* (New York, 1950), pp. ix–x.

12. Reid, p. 154.

13. West, "Some Notes on Violence," *Contact*, I (October 1932), p. 132.

The West and Eschatology

1. William Faulkner, *Light in August* (New York, 1950), p. 6; "Address Upon Receiving the Nobel Prize for Literature," in *The Portable Faulkner*, revised edition (New York, 1967), p. 724.

2. Perry Miller, *Errand Into the Wilderness* (New York, 1956), p. 217.

3. Henry Nash Smith, *Mark Twain's Fable of Progress: Political and Economic Ideas in "A Connecticut Yankee"* (New Brunswick, New Jersey, 1964), pp. 104, 94–95.

4. Mark Twain, *A Connecticut Yankee in King Arthur's Court* (New York, 1899), p. 404.

5. In Bernard DeVoto, *Mark Twain at Work* (Cambridge, Massachusetts, 1942).

6. Mark Twain, *Which Was the Dream? and Other Symbolic Writings of the Later Years*, ed. John S. Tuckey (Berkeley, 1967), p. 5.

7. Smith, p. 107.

8. Henry Adams, *The Degradation of the Democratic Dogma* (New York, 1958), pp. 177–179, 187.

9. Henry Adams, *Henry Adams and His Friends: A Collection of His Unpublished Letters*, ed. Harold Dean Cater (Boston, 1947), p. 292.

10. Henry Adams, *The Education of Henry Adams* (Boston, 1918), p. 435.

11. R. P. Blackmur, *The Expense of Greatness* (Gloucester, Massachusetts, 1958), p. 255.

12. Walt Whitman, *Leaves of Grass*, Comprehensive Readers' Edition, eds. Harold W. Blodgett and Sculley Bradley (New York, 1965), p. 731.

13. Dagobert D. Runes (ed.), *The Diary and Sundry Observations of Thomas Alva Edison* (New York, 1948), p. 239.

14. J. William Fulbright, *The Arrogance of Power* (New York, 1967), p. 4.

15. George Santayana, *Character and Opinion in the United States* (New York, 1956), p. 116.

Regionalism as Frontier Synthesis

1. Henry David Thoreau, *Walden* ("Higher Principles"); Ralph Waldo Emerson, "The Poet"; Walt Whitman, "Song of Myself."

2. Albert Camus, *The Myth of Sisyphus and Other Essays*, trans. Justin O'Brien (New York, 1959), pp. 20–21.

3. D. H. Lawrence, *Studies in Classic American Literature* (New York, 1953), pp. 16–17.

4. Hayden Carruth, "New England," in *Regional Perspectives*, ed. J. G. Burke (Chicago, 1973), p. 3.

5. Cecilio Blacktooth, in *Touch the Earth: A Self-Portrait of Indian Existence*, comp. T. C. McLuhan (New York, 1971), p. 28.

6. Chief Seattle, *Ibid.*, p. 30.

7. Wendell Berry, *Home Economics* (San Francisco, 1987), p. 108.

8. *Ibid.*, p. 50.

9. *Ibid.*, p. 107.

10. Yi-Fu Tuan, *Topophilia: A Study of Environmental Perception, Attitudes, and Values* (Englewood Cliffs, New Jersey, 1974), chap. 15.

11. *Ibid.*, pp. 124–125.

12. A similar schema, though having different developmental analysis, is found in Rufus A. Coleman, "Literature and the Region," *Pacific Northwest Quarterly*, XXXIX (October 1948), pp. 312–318. See also George Venn, "Continuity in Northwest Literature," in *Northwest Perspectives: Essays on the Culture of the Pacific Northwest*, eds. Edwin R. Bingham and Glenn A. Love (Eugene and Seattle, 1979), pp. 98–118.

13. William Stafford, "On Being Local," *Northwest Review*, XIII (1973), p. 92.

14. Don Berry, *Trask* (New York, 1960), p. 365.

15. Norman Maclean, *A River Runs Through It and Other Stories* (Chicago, 1976), p. 104.

16. *The Collected Poems of Theodore Roethke* (Garden City, New York, 1965), pp. 205, 239, 242, 250.

17. Kermit Vanderbilt, "Theodore Roethke as a Northwest Poet," in Bingham and Love (eds.), p. 215.

18. *Ibid.*, p. 214.

Three Montana Regionalists: Ivan Diog, James Welch, Norman Maclean

1. Ivan Doig, *This House of Sky: Landscapes of a Western Mind* (New York, 1978), p. 10.

2. James Welch, *Winter in the Blood* (New York, 1986), p. 19.

3. Frederick Turner, *Beyond Geography: The Western Spirit Against the Wilderness* (New York, 1980), p. 293.

4. Lionel Trilling, *Beyond Culture: Essays on Literature and Learning* (New York, 1968), pp. 8, 9.

5. Norman Maclean, *A River Runs Through It and Other Stories* (Chicago, 1976), p. 1.

Home and the Good Life

1. Wendell Berry, *Standing by Words* (San Francisco, 1983), p. 103. I am indebted to Berry for his discussion of the horizontal and the vertical.

2. *Ibid.*, p. 178.

3. *Ibid.*, pp. 3–23.

4. Ivan Doig, *Winter Brothers: A Season at the Edge of America* (New York, 1980), p. 241.

5. Theodore Roethke, "The Rose," in *Collected Poems* (New York, 1965), p. 205.

Index

Index

"Significance of the Frontier in American History" (Turner), 22–23, 25–26, 54
Simms, William Gilmore, 88
Sinclair, Upton, 105
"Sinners in the Hands of an Angry God" (Edwards), 124
Sister Carrie (Dreiser), 133
Smith, Henry Nash, 17–18, 21, 47, 55, 66–67, 68, 96, 126, 127, 129
Snyder, Gary, 7, 50, 51, 137
Sometimes a Great Notion (Kesey), 51
"Song of Myself" (Whitman), 24
"Soul has bandaged moments, The" (Dickinson), 11
Soul of the Far East, The (Lowell), 134
Spencer, Herbert, 56, 133
Spengemann, William C., 67
Spiritualism, 58, 133–135
Spoils of Poynton, The (James), 123
Spreckels, Claus, 24
Stafford, William, 145
Stegner, Wallace, 50, 174
Steinbeck, John, 50, 51, 105
Sterling, George, 51
Stevens, Isaac, 141
Story of My Boyhood and Youth, The (Muir), 42
Strenuous Life, The (Roosevelt), 95
Studies in Classic American Literature (Lawrence), 138–139
Styron, William, 123
Suckow, Ruth, 89
Sumner, Charles, 131

Taylor, Bayard, 102
"Tendency of History, The" (Adams), 131
Tennyson, Alfred, 21
Their Fathers' God (Rölvaag), 84, 96, 99–100

"Their Height in Heaven comforts not" (Dickinson), 11
This House of Sky (Doig), 148–155, 156
Thomson, William (Lord Kelvin), 129
Thoreau, Henry David: 2, 21, 23, 30, 38, 41, 53, 56, 132, 138, 174; "Civil Disobedience," 56; "Walking," 132–133
Tillich, Paul, 26
Tocqueville, Alexis de, 95
Tolstoy, Leo, 106
Tom Sawyer (Twain), 72
Trask (Berry), 146
Trilling, Lionel, 162–163
To Tullinger (*Two Fools*, later rev. to *Pure Gold*) (Rölvaag), 94
"Tragic, The" (Emerson), 5–6
Travels in Alaska (Muir), 37
Tuan, Yi-Fu, 143
Tuckey, John S., 129
Turner, Frederick, 143
Turner, Frederick Jackson: 1, 2, 16–27, 44–45, 53–55, 87, 102, 125, 126; "Contributions of the West to American Democracy," 24; "Poet of the Future, The," 20; "Problems in American History," 21–22; "Significance of History, The," 19, 20; "Significance of the Frontier in American History," 22–23, 25–26, 54; "West and American Ideals, The," 21
Twain, Mark: 2, 4, 12, 50, 65, 66–83, 95, 145, 165; *Adventures of Huckleberry Finn, The*, 12, 66–83, 116–117; *Connecticut Yankee in King Arthur's Court, A*, 12, 14, 126; "Enchanted Sea-Wilderness, The," 128–129; *Life on the Mississippi*, 75;